IB History Exam Study Guide

International Contemporary History 1848–2008

Dr. Juan R. Céspedes, Ph.D.

Cover: US Army tanks face off in the American Sector against Soviet armor at Checkpoint Charlie, Berlin, October 1961. US Army photo from the U.S. Army Military History Institute (MHI).

DEDICATION

To my wonderful father, Manuel Céspedes, in thanks for the love of history, international relations and social issues that he instilled in me. He accomplished this cleverly as we watched and discussed NBC's "Meet the Press", ABC's "Issues and Answers", and "CBS' Walter Cronkite" in our second hand, black and white, rabbit-eared television.

CONTENTS

"The purpose of life is to live to be one hundred, so that one is entitled to teach history from personal experience."

~ Dr. Juan R. Céspedes, during a lecture in 2005

CHAPTER 1
HOW TO USE THIS STUDY GUIDE

This study guide can be an extremely useful tool in helping you prepare for the IB History Exam. It is carefully constructed to help you review important topics and details. Think of it also as a template where you can highlight key points as you go on, information that you want to review further, or add your own ideas and data if you wish.

The International Baccalaureate history examination encompasses a broad range of information. The scope of the curriculum may make some students feel overwhelmed: DON'T BE. With this study guide you will traverse all the areas of the exam. They are as follows:

Paper One (part one of the exam), The prescribed subject area, "Communism in Crisis" covered here, is a document-based essay with four compulsory questions relating to the Soviet Union and Eastern Europe until 1991, or post 1976 China. You have 1 hour to complete this part of the exam.

Paper Two (part two of the exam) is essay based. Students are presented with six topic areas, and in each of these they are presented with five possible essay topic questions. Students only have to answer two questions in total, but they cannot be from within the same topic area. You have 1½ hours to complete the exam. The topic areas covered here are as follows:

1.   The Cold War
2.   Causes, Practices and Effects of War
3.   Nationalist and Independence Movements, Decolonialization and Challenges Facing New States
4.   The Rise and Rule of Single-Party States
5.   Peace and Cooperation: international organizations and multiparty states

Paper Three (part three of the exam) is taken by students taking the Higher Level History component. This paper is based on the history of a specific region (Regional Option), the exam is also essay based with students selecting three questions from a list of 24-25 on their region of choice. The region covered here is the Americas.

So you see, the IB History Exam is extremely doable, and especially so with this test prep!

Dr. Juan R. Céspedes, Ph.D.

CHAPTER 2

REVOLUTION & COUNTER-REVOLUTION 1848-1870

Europe faced a period of social, economic, and political turbulence in the middle of the 19th century that would have consequences that would reach into the 20th century.

- Never before had Europe seen such extensive revolutionary upheaval as it did in 1848

- People in Europe sought essentially the same goals:

  - Constitutional government

  - Independence and unification of national groups

  - End to serfdom and manorial restraints (where they still existed)

- Although the revolutions of 1848 were widespread, they generally lacked basic driving and strength, succumbing to military repression and leaving a legacy of class fears and conflicts.

- **Paris: The Specter of Social Revolution in the West**

- The interests of the few interests were represented in legislative bodies (where they existed)

- Basic issues were seldom debated

- Corruption was prevalent and fraud was constant

- Radicals wanted universal male suffrage and a republic

- Liberals wanted broadening of voting rights within the existing constitutional monarchy

- **In France,** King Louis Philippe and Prime Minister François Guizot opposed any meaningful change to the status quo.

- **The "February" Revolution in France**

- Reformers planned a demonstrations in February 1848; the government forbade such meetings

- Barricades were built by the insurgents in the streets, and the government called out the National Guard; the insurgents refused to move

- The King promised electoral reform, but it was too late: Republican "firebrands" took charge of the semi-mobilized working class

- February 24th Louis Philippe abdicated
- Republican leaders set up a provisional government of 10 men before the election of the Constituent Assembly
- **What is a provisional government? We will see them set up many times throughout history!**
    - A **provisional government** is an emergency or interim government set up when a political void has been created by the collapse of an institutional but ineffective government.
- The provisional government had 7 "political" Republicans (headed by Alphonse de Lamartine) and 3 "social" Republicans (headed by Louis Blanc)
- Louis Blanc (his socialist ideas are a portent of things to come in the 20th century)
    - Wanted a bold economic and social program soon
    - Wanted a Ministry of Progress; "social workshops" supported by the state
    - Wanted collectivist manufacturing establishments
    - Got the creation of a Labor Commission (it actually had no power); managed to abolish slavery in French colonies but didn't get a 10 hour work day approved
    - Got National Workshops
- National Workshops
    - Extensive project of unemployment relief
    - Women were excluded; men were sent to build road and fortifications outside of Paris
    - There were too many men for the amount of work available (200,000 people by June 1848)
- The Constituent Assembly (elected by universal male suffrage) ends up replacing the Provisional Government with an executive board that included no "social" Republicans; Lamartine was in charge
- Revolutionary leaders in Paris were unwilling to accept the processes of majority rule or slow parliamentary deliberation
- **The "June Days" of 1848**
- Working-class agitators attacked the Constituent Assembly, announcing the need for a social revolution; they set up a new provisional government
- National Guard restores the Constituent Assembly; they now want to root out socialism by getting rid of National Workshops
    - Workers enrolled in the National Workshops had three choices: join the army, transfer to provincial workshops, or leave the country
- Laboring class resisted, the government proclaims martial law, and power handed over to the army
- "Bloody June Days"- men from workshops (numbering 20,000) took up arms
- Class war had broken out, bourgeoisie and upper classes were worried

- Chartist movement in England is revived as a result
    - Movement by working-class laborers for political and social reform in Great Britain
    - Violent English minority of radical workers and journalists
- **The Emergence of Louis Napoleon Bonaparte**
- After the June days, Constituent Assembly decides to draft a republican constitution and set up government.
- Aiming for a strong government
- Grant universal male suffrage
- Candidates for President:
- Lamartine - wants vaguely moral and idealistic republic (18,000 votes)
- Cavaignac - wanted republic of discipline and order (1,500,000 votes)
- Ledru-Rollin - held chastened social ideas (370,000 votes)
- Bonaparte - although his views weren't very clear he gains 5,400,000 votes and becomes the WINNER!
- Louis Napoleon Bonaparte
    - Born 1808
    - Son of Louis Bonaparte, King of Holland; grandson of the infamous Napoleon
    - When Louis Napoleon comes to power in Holland after his father dies in 1832, he fails to seize Strasbourg (1836) and Boulogne (1840)
    - Gets sentenced to life in prison in fortress of Ham; escapes dressed as a stonemason (1846)
    - Joined Carbonari (secret Italian revolutionary societies) and was a part of Italian revolution and uprisings in 1830
    - Wrote two books: *Napoleonic Ideas* (defending his uncle) and *Extinctions of Poverty* (anti-capitalist)
    - Opposed Chartism
    - Wanted to be benevolent towards common people while maintaining order
- **If no one knew his platform, then why did he win?** He was very popular among members of the peasantry and lower classes who lacked any sense of political efficacy.
- May 1849, the Constituent Assembly is replaced by the Legislative Assembly
- Royalist majority
- 2/3 monarchists (1/2 are Legitimists (favor Charles X line), ½ are Orleantists (favor Louis Philippe line)
- 1/3 republicans (3/4 socialists, ¼ old-fashioned republicans)

(For the more visual-learners)

The Legislative Assembly

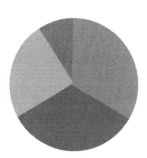

- Monarchists (Legitimists)
- Monarchists (Orleantists)
- Socialists
- Republicans

- Napoleon and the Assembly wished to expel socialism's association with republicanism
- He ousts socialist deputies, banned public meetings, abolished universal male suffrage so the lower classes couldn't vote (1850)
- Falloux Law of 1850 - schools must be under supervision of Catholic clergy
- Thus, the French government became anti-republican
- However, Bonaparte still wanted the support of the radicals who were outraged by the abolishment of universal male suffrage; Bonaparte re-establishes it in 1851
- Then, he turns against the Assembly by convincing everyone they are "greedy plutocrats"
- December 2nd, 1851- Napoleon executes a coup d' etat, dissolving the Assembly and causing France to lack a parliament form of government
- Napoleon is elected to a 10-year term by the people
- Republic is DEAD due to radicalism
- Liberalism and constitutionalism were DEAD as well
- **Vienna: The Nationalist Revolution in Central Europe and Italy**
- **The Austrian Empire in 1848**
- Ruled by the Hapsburgs
- Capital is Vienna
- Most populous European state besides Russia
- 3 regions:
  - Austria
  - Hungary
  - Bohemia
- Also included Venetia and Lombardy
- Germans- leaders of Austria

- Czechs- occupy Bohemia and Morovia
- Magyars- occupy Hungary, take pride in unique language
- Slavs- included Czechs, Poles, Ruthenians, Slovaks, Serbs, Croats, Slovenes, Dalmatians
- Romanians- take pride in linguistic similarities to Latins in the West
- Milan (Lombardy)- center of trade
- Bohemia- textiles
- Influence of Hapsburgs felt throughout Europe
- *Volkgeist* (cultural nationalism) was evident as liberalism spread
- Prince Klemens Wenzel von Metternich believed that extreme nationalism would divide the Austrian Empire, but he did nothing about it; said it would produce "the war of all against all"
- Fundamental problem of Austrian Empire: uniting people under a common government
- Metternich believed that a supreme government and bureaucracy should rule over the people, with whom it needs no connection and who don't need a connection with each other (this is better suited for a local government or agricultural society, NOT an empire)
- **The March Days**
- News of the February Revolution in Paris brought Magyar nationalist Lajos Kossuth to the fore in Hungary.
- His speech in Budapest was heard in Vienna, it drove Metternich from power.
- Rioting in Berlin led the King of Prussia to promise a constitution
- Hungary claimed autonomy within the Empire
- Status was granted to Bohemia by Emperor Ferdinand.
- Milan and Venetia declared their independence and the people of Florence declared their republic.
- The King of Piedmont-Sardinia declared war on Austria and invaded northern Italy.
- **The Turning of the Tide after June**
- The revolutionaries were poorly organized
- They were men of ideas, not spokesmen or powerful interests.
- Workers were not politically conscious, they soon separated into factions.
- The army was the key it had noble officers and peasant troops.
- Germans had an all-German assembly in May for Frankfort
- The Czechs had an all-Slavic assembly in Prague in June.
- The Czech assembly was anti-German
- Not anti-Austrian or anti-Habsburg.
    - Bohemia divided the Sudeten Germans and the Czechs.

- - In Vienna, a mass insurrection forced Emperor Ferdinand to flee.
  - Forces of counter-revolution = the landed nobility, the Catholic clergy, and the arm
- Brought Francis Joseph to the throne.
- **The Final Outburst and Repression, 1849**
- Riots, insurrections continued in 1849
- Mazzini established a republic in Rome
- Kossuth declared Hungary independent
- The Austrian army crushed Italy, with Russian troops called to stop the Hungarians.
- Pius IX condemned liberalism.
- Austria became repressive under the Bach system:
- The government was rigidly centralized, peasants were emancipated, internal trade barriers were ended, and administrative efficiency was increased.
- **The German States**
- The Frankfurt Assembly met from May 1848 to May 1849
- It brought a liberal, constitutional government to a united Germany.
- The collapse of the existing German governments made it possible in the March days of 1848.
- Austria claimed historic rights in the region
- Prussia was composed of the Rhineland, the area around Berlin, West Prussia, Posen, and East Prussia.
- Prussia was controlled by the Junkers
- **Berlin: Failure of the Revolution in Prussia**
- Prussia was not democratic but not backward.
- Its government was efficient, progressive and fair.
  - High literacy, university and elementary school system.
  - Created a Zollverein, which was a coalition of German states formed to manage customs and economic policies.
  - Berlin riots had led to the creation of a legislative assembly
  - The Assembly was dominated by anti-Junker lower-class extremists who were also anti-Russian.
    - They set up new pro-Polish institutions in Posen (which were later destroyed)
- **The Frankfurt Assembly**
- German voters elected delegates, but the Assembly was still weak since it represented nothing but an idea
- It had no power to issue orders or force compliance
- No army or civil service to act.

- The Assembly was professional, middle class
- It opposed violence and revolution, opposed working class upheaval.
- Radicals rioted in Frankfurt; the Assembly called in the Prussian army to suppress them.
- The Assembly divided into:
  - Great Germans, wanting union under the Austrian Emperor
  - Little Germans, wanting to exclude Austria and unify under the King of Prussia.
- In Frankfurt, a constitution is written, speaking of the "rights of Germans" and offered the throne to Frederick William IV, he refused to take it.
- Frederick William issued the Prussian Constitution of 1850.
- It called for a parliament with two chambers.
- **The New Toughness of Mind: Realism, Positivism, Marxism**
- The "springtime of peoples" (revolutions of 1848) had failed.
- Constitutional liberty was secured for a few small states, but national freedom had not been gained nor had democracy been advanced.
- Serfdom had ended: peasants were free to move, find new jobs, take part in a money economy, or migrate (but once freed, peasants showed little concern for constitutional or bourgeois ideas).
- The main result was a new toughness of mind. Idealism was discredited; radicals were less optimistic, conservatives more willing to be repressive. Industries developed, times were prosperous; prices and wages were rising, property owners felt secure, and labor leaders turned from theories to organizing viable unions, especially for skilled trades.
- **Materialism, Realism, Positivism**
- According to materialism, the spiritual, mental, or ideal grew from the physical world. Romanticism was replaced by realism in literature and art
- Theory that one should describe life as it was.
- Trust in science was combined with religious skepticism
- Opposing organized religion to the radical notion that religion was an invention to aid the "haves."
- Positivism was the philosophy of French philosopher Auguste Comte
  - Comte called for a new social doctrine based on the sciences. He was a major influence to 19th century thought, impacting the work of social thinkers such as Karl Marx, John Stuart Mill, and George Eliot
- The function of sociology, the science of society, was to determine the laws of social progress.
- Politics - the new attitude was called *realpolitik, which* was the politics of reality.
- Governments should be orderly, hard working, and honest.
- **Marxism**

10

- Karl Marx (1818-1883) was the son of a lawyer in the Rhineland.
- 1848 he met Friedrich Engels (1820-1893), son of a German textile manufacturer with a plant in Manchester.
- They joined the Communist League in Paris in 1847
- Agitated for a radical socialist revolutionary program for Germany.
- Their program alarmed the Frankfurt Assembly.
- It was in this connection that Marx and Engels wrote their **Communist Manifesto** in 1848.
- <u>Sources and Content of Marxism</u>: merged German philosophy, French revolutionary thought, British industrial revolution
- Marx developed idea of alienation of labor: social experience and state of mind produced when humans in process of mechanization become estranged from objects on which they work
    - Distinctive feature of modern capitalist society
    - Marx believed that freedom would happen only when private property and capital is abolished
- Engels published *The Condition of the Working Classes in England*: essentially the same conclusions as Marx
    - Capital goods, government/parliament is in hands of wealthy
    - Religion held lower classes in servile obedience ("Opium of the masses")
    - Family was disintegrating in the cities (living conditions, exploitations of women/children)
        - These thoughts are dramatized in *Communist Manifesto*: call to revolution; confirmed beliefs it was just huge class struggle; workers should be loyal only to their own class
        - Marx's *Capital*
            - Subsistence theory of wages (Iron Law): workers will never have more than minimum wage
            - Labor theory of value: value of object depends on amount of labor put into it
            - Doctrine of surplus value: the value created by workers in excess of their own labour-cost, was appropriated by the capitalist as gross profit, thus workers were being robbed
                - Theory of Dialectical Materialism: history is shaped by impersonal forces and deep structural changes caused by class struggle, rather than individuals or chance events
                - Hegel emphasizes ideas as a cause of social change, but Marx emphasizes material conditions and relations of production
            - Marx's theory of historical development (Dialectical Materialism):

- Every economy in history grows while simultaneously developing internal contradictions and weaknesses that contribute to its systemic decay
- Material conditions shape economic classes
- Classes develop their own ideology
- Classes clash: bourgeoisie revolutions vs. feudal interests
- Bourgeoisie compete and destroy each other until only a few are left, others become proletariat
- Proletariat masses take over the bourgeoisie
- Social revolution!
- Dictatorship of proletariat (war between proletariat and bourgeoisie)
- State and religion will eventually disappear and pure communist society develop

- Other important ideas of Marx and Hegel
  - Government is instrument of class power
  - Religion is the "opium of the masses", meant to assuage workers and keep the wealthy classes and oppressive capitalist governments in power.
  - Worker solidarity: workers must lose themselves in the whole – it is a crime to improve their social position; do not put faith in social legislation

- **Appeal of Marxism**
  - Advantage: claimed to be scientific and not utopian
  - Weakness: working class not devoted to Marxist ideas
  - Instead of listening to Marx, after revolutions of 1848, workers engage in "opportunism": better themselves by cooperating with employers. Marx is against this – his ideas are not promoting revolutionary fervor (for now!)

- <u>**Bonapartism and the 2nd French empire 1852-1870**</u>
- **Political Institutions**
- Napoleon III came to power because of fear of radicalism in a republic
- Advocated modern progress:
  - Sovereignty of the people
  - Thought parliament accentuated class differences
  - Wanted to govern equally over all classes
    - Authoritarian political institutions:
      - Council of State: draft legislations
      - Appointive Senate
      - Legislative Body (universal male suffrage) – no independent powers

- **Economic Developments**

- Favorable times for expansion
- Increased prices encourage capital investment (more railroads, Suez Canal) – start of modern imperialism
- Large corporations emerge – limited liability
- Humanitarian relief of suffering: hospitals, asylums, free medicines (like social-welfare)
- Napoleon suspected of being socialist
- Wanted free international trade: reduction of import duties.
- **Internal Difficulties and War**
- Made enemies from free trade policy
- 1860s: decade of Liberal Empire
- Crimean War will ruin Napoleon

CHAPTER 3

MODERN NATION STATES FORM & CONSOLIDATE

Backgrounds: The Idea of the Nation-State

- Before 1860, Great Britain and France were most powerful European countries
- Small states compromised fragments of a nation
- Consolidation of large nations became a model for other states (large and small)
- Small and middle class-sized populations through themselves
- Idea of nation-states served to bring people together into larger units and breaking them into smaller ones
- In the 19th century, nationalism became a "secular faith"
- Nation-state: supreme authority somehow rests upon and represents the will and feeling of its inhabitants
  - o Must see themselves as part of a community
  - o The government is *their* government
  - o Nation may consist of people who speak same language, have common descent, future, religion, etc
  - o All are alike in the feeling of being a community committed to a collective destiny of each
- Phases of consolidation of large nation-states
  - o Territorially-union of preexisting smaller states
  - o Morally and psychologically- creation of new ties between gov't and governed and admission of new segments of population to an established political life
- **Crimean War**
- Crimean War helped make possible the success of European national movements
- Severely weakened both Russia and Austria
- First war to be covered by newspaper correspondents
- First war in which women established position as army nurses
- 1853: dispute between Russia and Turkey regarding protection of Christians in Ottoman Empire

- - France claimed to protect them too
- Napoleon 3 hated Russian Tsar b/c he said he was radical
- France encourages Turkey to resist Russian claims
- FR and GB and Sardinia sided with Turkey; invade Crimean peninsula in Russia
- Austrian empire wanted to prevent encroachment, cause Russians to evacuate
- Tsar Nicholas dies in 1855
- Russia gave up territory
- Congress of Paris = PEACE
- Trouble still coming…
- **Cavour and the Italian War of 1859: The Unification of Italy**
- The governments of each nation-stare enjoyed their sovereignty, yet they were too separate from the people who they governed.
- However, there was a growing desire for a liberal, national, united Italy that could be resurrected to the same political greatness as it experienced during the Renaissance
- **Camillo di Cavour**, the **ruler of Piedmont**, tried to make his state a model of progress, efficiency, and fairness in government
  - Wanted railroads, wanted to improve agriculture, and promoted free trade
- **Cavour** was extremely anticlerical, **had no sympathy for radical Mazzini, shared a toughness if mind (VERY IMPORTANT)**; and believed in the politics of reality.
- Joins **Crimean War** to get **Italian Question of unification** discussed at **Congress of Vienna**
- Cavour sees that Mazzini screwed up, so he decides he'll give the whole unification thing a shot; Napoleon hops on the bandwagon
- So then Cavour decides to trick Austria (remember, they're weak right now) into declaring war on Piedmont
- French army helps defeat them, but then Prussia mobilized on the Rhine and people are rebelling all over Italy after they managed to beat the Austrians
- Napoleon and his Catholic friends fear that the pope is going to lose power, so they encourage him to make peace with Austria
- Each Italian state had finally been recognized by **Napoleon III** and by the **Congress of Paris (1856)**
- At the end of the war, the Franco-Austrian agreement gave Lombardy to Piedmont.
- Then, the Italian states of the North get annexed to Piedmont.
- France recognized Piedmont in exchange for Nice and Savoy; unification begins!
- By making peace with Austria, the Italian Question of unity was essentially answered
  - As for the issue if Garibaldi, who tried to use his control of Sicily to encroach upon Rome, his control of the kingdom of two Sicily's was

usurped by a unanimous decision of the people to be annexed to Piedmont.

- In 1861, the kingdom of Italy was declared, with Victor Emmanuel II as king. To complete unification, Italy annexed Venetia in 1866 and Rome in 1870.

- **Bismarck: The Found of a German Empire**

- Germans become dissatisfied with their position

- Become nationalistic after Napoleonic Wars

- Emphasize progressive evolution of history

- In **1862, Otto Von Bismarck** was appointed Prime Minister of PRUSSIA

- Bismarck wants to enlarge Prussia; Denmark moves to annex Schleswig, the Diet of the German Confederation calls for war against them and joins Austria (**1864**)

- Prussia & Austria win!
  o Prussia gets **Schleswig**
  o Austria gets **Holstein....causes problems later**

- Bismarck isolates Austria after war, becomes allies with Russia who disliked Austria still because of the Crimean War, and promised Venetia to Italy

- Bismarck attempted to pry Holstein away from Austria diplomatically, and when Austria refused he prepared for battle (**1867**)

- The Prussian army was well trained and armed with the new rapid-fire needle gun, and moved rapidly by the new railroads.

- **von Moltke -** commanded the Prussian army and led them in overthrowing the Austrians at the **Battle of Sadowa**

- The war was over and peace made before the rest of Europe knew what was happening. **(ALSO KNOWN AS THE SEVEN WEEK'S WAR)**

- 1867- Bismarck organized the North German Confederation- it enlarged Prussia joined with 21 other states

- Bismarck, the chief minister of Prussia, proposed a constitution for the North German Confederation which he intended to be stronger than the former confederation formed in 1815.

- Bismarck also ensured that this new government would be democratic and would be preferable for the people, since he believed that the people are an ally to the strong government against private interest

    o King of Prussia would be in charge, ministers were responsible to him

    o Parliament with two chambers

    o Bismarck takes over Paris with the defeat of the French in the Franco-Prussian War in 1870 and **proclaimed the German Empire January 18th, 1871**

- **The Dual Monarchy of Austria-Hungary**

- Its creation revised what had been established by the Peace's if Vienna and Westphalia.

- By industrializing heavily around 1870, it became the most powerful country in Europe.
- The new all-German state was dominated by Prussia and excluded Austria; exactly what Bismarck wanted.
- Prussian liberals capitulated, leaving conservatives like Bismarck in control.
- There was an established Reichstag elected by universal male suffrage, making the empire seem democratic and quelling any rebellions, thus allowing the empire to be strong.
- Each region maintained its form of government while giving the King of Prussia complete power over the military and all foreign policy for the whole empire.
- Liberalism withered away as nationalism took hold and made them stronger
- It was the rulers who joined the empire, not the people · When Bismarck united Germany, he left out 1/6th of the German population in Bohemia and Austria.
- The Magyars of Hungary felt that the Germanic influence was very oppressive (they always had problem with nationalism, see Chapter 12)
- In 1867, Austria and Hungary decided to set their differences aside and form a dual monarchy with the Ausgleich.
    - The Leith River divided them: east of it was Hungary, west of it was Austria
    - Each had their own constitution and their own parliament and would not intervene in the affairs of one another
    - Austrian nat'l language was German, Hungarian nat'l language was Magyar
    - The ways in which they were joined would be that they had the same Hapsburg ruler to be emperor of Austria and king of Hungary and have several common ministries
- Essentially, they treated each other as if each was sovereign but were still linked in ways that would benefit both nation-states.
- However, those who were not German or Magyarian got screwed over by this deal
    - the people in Hungary who owned estates dominated everything
    - lower classes (agrarian peasants) composed of Serbs and Slovaks
    - no true universal male suffrage was instituted until 1907
- **Liberalization in Tsarist Russia: Alexander II**
- As Tsar, Alexander II cultivated liberal support and overcame revolutionary anarchists.
- He gave people the opportunity to travel outside of Russia, eased control on schools, and decreased censorship.
- These liberal reforms allowed for an outburst of public opinion free of persecution.
- With the Act of Emancipation freeing the peasants in 1861, revolutionaries were outraged.
- The dissatisfied intelligentsia called themselves "nihilists," meaning they believed in nothing but science.

- They gained the support of peasants who were dissatisfied by having to pay large redemption taxes.

- Alexander II made more liberal reforms like abolishing the secret police and gave more freedom to the press.

- The anarchist Bakunin, and his disciple Nechaiev, called for terrorism against all who stood in the way, including liberals

- However, he was assassinated by the People's Will, a revolutionary group. Thus, he failed to overcome the anarchists.

- **The United States: The American Civil War**

- 1830s, Alexis de Tocqueville saw a future of rapid growth and change for the United States and predicted great power for the nation by 1900.

- In 1860, the US population (31 million) surpassed Britain's and nearly equaled that of France due to a high birth rate and increasing immigration from northern and western Europe.

- The US lacked minorities in a European sense; newcomers were willing to adopt English and embrace American national attitudes--traditions of republicanism and self-government, of individual liberty, free enterprise, and economic opportunity.

- The US was divided between the North, with its factories and need for tariffs, and the agricultural South, serving Europe with its cotton and importing needed goods.

- The South was deeply involved in slavery and the plantation system at the time when it had been abolished in the colonies of Britain and France and in the Latin American republics.

- The drive west brought the competition into the open, with a fragile peace maintained by the Compromise of 1820 ("Missouri Compromise") and the Compromise of 1850.

- Southern nationalism was emerging like that of the Magyars--states' rights with an aristocratic ethical code, the demand for independence and the freedom to control subject peoples.

- The Republican party offered a northern program: a west of small farmers, developed railroads, and high tariffs--and the threat of a radical abolitionism; the result was the Civil War.
    - European governments were partial to the South, though most workers were pro-North.
    - France and Great Britain saw advantages in the break-up of the Union.
    - The victory of the North brought the complete rule of central authority over states.

- The 14th Amendment secured the concept by forbidding any state to "deprive any person of life, liberty or property without due process of law"--a due process determined by the national government.

- Slavery was abolished, without compensation — an unprecedented seizure of private property.

- Radical Republicans wanted the reconstruction of the South, and for a period similar to the most advanced phase of the French Revolution, the national

18

government and army forced liberty and equality on a recalcitrant South under conditions of emergency rule.

- o The program finally ran out of steam and was abandoned in the 1870s, and the Southern whites regained control in a counterrevolution.
- The war had brought northern expansion--financiers, bankers, builders, manufacturers, protected by the Morrill Tariff.
- The Union Pacific railroad was incorporated, partly as a war measure in 1861, and the trans-continental railroad was completed in 1869.
- The Homestead Act made possible the settling of the West, with cheap land and the development of land-grant colleges.
- The Fourteenth Amendment was seen as protecting property rights rather than human rights, and industry boomed--complete with corruption, graft, speculation, and other minor forms of dishonesty
- **The Dominion of Canada**
- **France vs. Britain**
- Divided between French (Quebec, St. Lawrence Valley) and English (Loyalists in Maritime Provinces and recent immigrants in Ontario)
- French opposed assimilation – Quebec Act 1774 gave toleration to French language, culture and religion
- 1791: Britain wants to create 2 self-governing provinces: Upper Canada (English) and Lower Canada (French), but French fear English minority, and English fear the new immigrants, and blockage of trade
- War of 1812 increases national sentiment
- Fighting in 1837
- Reform Whigs send Earl of Durham the "Durham Report": unified Canada with virtual self-government and "responsible government" (elected assembly and ceremonial figure of governor). This is accepted, but French still fear continuing English migration
- British North America Act 1867: creates Dominion of Canada as federation (both centralizes and decentralizes!)
  - o Ruled by common parliament with responsible government
  - o First successful example of devolution (granting of political freedom): leads to ultimate peace settlement of colonialism in Asia/Africa after WWII
  - o Stabilizes relations between British North America and the U.S
- **Japan and the West**
- **Background**
- Since 1600, self-imposed isolation to establish and stabilize own dynasty and prevent European penetration
  - o Tokugawa clan controlled shogunate (military head) – tried to stop Christian and western penetration
  - o Japan is sealed off by 1640: only trade was with Dutch in Nagasaki

- Tokugawa's government was centralized but still feudal
- Daimyo (lords) and samurai (warriors) are landed aristocracy. They become indebted to merchants
- Distinct class lines (different taxes, clothing, and punishment)
- Secularized society – Buddhism is losing control
    - Emphasis on Bushido ("way of warrior"): stressed honor and loyalty
    - Shintoism reemerged: emperors are seen as true sons of heaven – shogunates are just usurpers
        - Western goods/ideas trickle in – Japan has more access to west than vice versa

- **Opening of Japan**
- Commodore Perry arrives in 1853
- Many people want to westernize: entrepreneurial nobles, poor samurai wanting a new job, merchants, scholars, westernizing patriots
- Signed unequal treaties
    - Extra-territoriality: Europeans and Americans in Japan are still under western jurisdiction
    - Western control of Japanese tariffs
        - Japanese lords want to drive out western influence, but bombardments of lords of Satsuma and Choshu prove Japan is weakness
            - These lords decide to westernize rapidly
            - Force Shogun to resign in 1867
            - The start of Meiji Era: time of rapid change
- **Meiji Era (1868-1912) – westernization of Japan**
- Goal: learn the west's secrets in order to defend itself
    - Reforms:
        - Feudal system abolished – becomes a modern nation-state!
        - Legal system reorganized: equality before the law, no more "barbaric" punishments for criminals
        - Reformed military (based on Prussian army and British navy)
        - Centralized monetary system, national postal system, national school system (increases literacy)
        - Buddhism was discouraged – replaced by Shintoism
        - Constitution written, called for parliament
        - Civil liberties and 2-chamber parliament
        - Emperor only had power in theory. In reality, ministers were free to rule based on what they thought was best for the state.

- Economy:
    - Foreign loans to supply new technologies
    - Increased foreign trade (and population!)
    - Industrial and financial modernization: becomes dependent on exports/imports to sustain living
- **Summary – the "Big Picture" in 1871**
    - Great Powers are Britain, France, Austria-Hungary, and Russia (obviously this changes a SUBSTANTIALLY in the next 50 years)
        - Canada became the daughter nation of Britain
        - No one knew what would happen in Italy or Japan
        - U.S.' role is increasing, but it's not as important as it will be in the near future

CHAPTER 4

THE ECONOMY & POLITICS OF EUROPEAN CIVILIZATION

Materialistic and Nonmaterialistic Ideals

- Europe= politically divided BUT all shared materialistic ideas about civilization
- Europe, US, Canada, Australia and New Zealand all thought they were part of the "civilized world"
  - Believed it was "well deserved after centuries of progress"
  - Believed in themselves as the most advanced people on Earth and felt that all others should respect them in the same way
    - Those who didn't adopt European ideas and technology were deemed "backward"
- All other zones considered "backward"
  - Asia
  - Africa
  - Latin America
- **NOTE: THESE IDEAS HELPED SHAPE IMPERIALISM IN THE 20th CENTURY**
- Why was 1900 better than 1800? **(materialistically)**
  - Higher standard of living
  - Well nourished & dressed well
  - Slept in softer beds
  - Better sanitation
- Being knowledgeable was also seen as part of being "civilized"
  - Science vs. dogmatism
  - Geographical knowledge
- Isaac Taylor wrote *Ulitimate Civilization,* published in **1860**, defined the moral ideal of eradicating barbarism as necessary to become a modern civilization; eliminate:
  - Polygamy
  - Prostitution **(more or less tolerated in all of Europe)**
  - Divorce

- o Sanguinary & immoral games
- o Torture **(generally out of use by 1800)**
- o Caste & slavery
- England, France, Sweden: **mortality rate fell** (the number of deaths)
- **Infant mortality rate** also fell in all countries affected by medical science
- Rise in **life expectancy**
- **Literacy rate** approached 100% in Europe
- **Productivity of labor** was greater in the more modern, industrialized countries
- **The "Zones" of Civilization**
- Two Europes: **Inner Zone and Outer Zone**
  - o **Inner Zone**
    - ▪ Great Britain, France, Belgium, Germany, Northern Italy, Western Austria
      - Extensive railroads
      - Heavy industry
      - Wealthier people seen through higher living standards and accumulation of capital
      - Strength of constitutional governments and parliaments **(example: GB, FR, IT)**
      - High labor productivity
      - **Similar to Northeast USA**
  - o **Outer Zone**
    - ▪ Most of Ireland, Iberian peninsula (Spain + Portugal), Italian peninsulas, anything east of Germany
      - Agricultural (sold livestock, lumber, grain, wool to the industrialized inner zone)
      - Poor, illiterate, died young
      - Wealthy people were absentee landlords
    - ▪ Borrowed capital from London & Paris, philosophies from Germany & the west, workers (technicians) to build bridges
    - ▪ **Similar to Southern USA and Latin America**
- **Third Zone:** beyond Europe was the "backwards" world of Asia and Africa (except Japan); these nations would become dependent upon Europe after 1870
- **European and World Population Growth since 1650**
- Proportion of Europeans in the world's total reached its maximum of all time between 1850 and WW2
- The organization of sovereign states finally subsided after 1871, so the period of civil wars and violence finally ended **(fewer wars resulted in political stability and population growth)**

- Less insecurity concerning agriculture and family life
- **Japan**: Tokugawa shogunate kept peace
- **China**: Manchu & Qing brought order
- **India (ruled by Britain) and Java (ruled by Dutch)**: European rule helped curb famine and violence
- Death rates fell, people lived longer, birth rate fell (more about this later)
- **CONTRASTS**
    - **Africa**: slave trade, 10 million slaves removed violently from their towns, disrupted African culture
    - **U.S.**: Native Americans devastated by disease
- **17th and 18th century:** Subsiding of bubonic plague and smallpox due to vaccination (invented by Edward Jenner)
- Agricultural improvements and new technologies (reaper, etc.) allowed for more food production, less famine
- Improvements in transportation (roads, canals, trains) allowed for food to be transported to areas in shortage
- By 1900, there was better drinking water and better sewage disposal in cities
- From **1650 and 1900**, European population **increased by a fourfold (x4)**
- **Stabilization of European Population**
- **Birth rate decreased**
    - Indicated a modern civilization
    - Families averaged about 2 to 4 children
    - Reflected new "small family system": reduced the birth rate using **contraception**
    - Why did they want smaller families?
        - Europeans married later, leaving less years for women to give birth
        - In France, Napoleonic Code stated that inheritances must be divided between all children; fewer children meant more money per child, and each child maintained a higher social status like their parents
    - **High economic security and possession of a high social standard** led to a reduction in the European birth rate
- In crowded cities, a small family made activities and life a whole lot easier for everyone in the family
- 70% of European working-class people were using contraception by the 1930's compared to 20% in 1900
- More people lived on into the middle and older age groups due to increased life expectancy!
- **Growth of Cities and Urban Life**

- Rural populations of the inner zone became more dense, but out of 7 people, 1 would leave the continent, 5 would go to cities, and only 1 would remain in their rural domain
- Railroads made it possible for there to be concrete manufacturing in large towns where foods and fuel could be moved to in great volume
- Germany began to rival England after 1870 in modern industrialization
- City life
    - Impersonal and anonymous
    - Lacked deference for aristocrats
    - Lacked sense of self-help
    - News spread fast (yellow journalism in 1900)
    - Disrespectful towards traditions
    - Receptive to new ideas (spread of socialism)
    - Made for a more alert and more informed public due to schools, access to books and newspapers, and extensive discussion among neighbors and city-folk
    - In crowded cities, a small family made activities and life easier for everyone in the family
- **<u>EXTENSIVE MIGRATION FROM EUROPE TO OTHER PARTS OF THE WORLD</u>**
- Almost 60 million people left Europe while cities grew
- **Atlantic Migration**
    - it was by the means of crossing the Atlantic Ocean that earlier colonies of Europe were transformed into new "mini-Europes"
- Most immigrants between 1850 and 1914 were from England, Italy, and Russia
- Groups who emigrated were not accurately represented in statistics
- After 1850 black slaves were still smuggled into US and Brazil
- Where did everyone go?
    - **British and Irish:** Canada and USA
    - **Italians:** USA and Latin America
    - **Spaniards:** Spanish American republics
    - **Portuguese:** Brazil
    - **Germans:** US (some to Argentina and Brazil)
- Half of all migration between 1850 and 1940 was to the United States
- Why did everyone leave?
    - Before 1914, the new countries welcomed immigration
        - It meant more workers to build houses, farm land, dig mines
    - Steamship travel made it easy and cheap to cross the sea
    - Railroads helped people to get to ports

- A rush of immigrants competing for jobs at low wages was undesirable economically, leading to the US establishing laws restricting immigration in the US
    - Emergency Quota Act of 1921 restricted annual immigration from a given country to 3% of the number of people from that country living in the U.S. in 1910
    - Immigration Act of 1924 aimed at freezing the current ethnic distribution in response to rising immigration from Southern and Eastern Europe, as well as from Asia.
    - People migrated to improve their living circumstances
    - **Irish Potato Famine (1845-1849):** 1.5 million Irish moved to US
    - **WWI:** Jews flee from Russia and Germany to escape persecution (pogroms)
    - For the first time, people had substantially increased freedom to move around
        - Disappearance of serfdom
        - European governments that allowed emigration
    - This migration took place at people's private initiative and private expense: economic independence!
    - **Industrial Advances:**
- **Before 1870**
    - Steam power
    - Growth of textile and metallurgical industries
    - Expansion of railroads
- Steam engine gets refined and improved
- Invention of internal combustion (gas) engine and diesel engine gave the world **automobiles, airplanes, and submarines.**
    - This makes **oil production** very important!
- **Telephone** invented by Alexander Gram Bell in 1870
- **Wireless signals** were transported across the Atlantic in **1901 (Marconi)**
- **Medical breakthroughs** (elimination of yellow fever, x-rays invented)
- **Refinement of iron** improved, allowing greater steel production (important for industrial age)
- **Railroad mileage multiplied**
- **Industry in Europe**
    - Britain, Germany, France become **INDUSTRIAL SUPERPOWERS**
        - Produced over 4/5of all European steel, coal, and machinery
- **By 1914**
    - American steel production was outproducing the three powers combine
    - American mechanization was ahead of Europe

- ▪ Pioneered assembly-line production (courtesy of Henry Ford and his automobile production techniques)
- With the Industrial Revolution in Europe, trading the goods produced there with nations around the world became a necessity to help create profits
- **Britain** proposes **free trade** with the **repeal of the <u>Corn Laws</u> (trade barriers designed to protect cereal/grain production in GB against competition from foreign inputs, mercantilist) in <u>1846</u>**
  - ○ Decide to become dependent upon overseas imports for food
- **France** adopts **free trade policies** in **<u>1860</u>**
- Europe was economically liberal, having conditions in which business was free from the political state, and remaining predominantly international!
- **All European countries imported more than they exported** (except Russia, Austria-Hungary, and the Balkan states)
  - ○ **Britain** led this trend; having an import surplus of about ¾ of 1 billion dollars a year before 1914
- Governments and businesses borrowed money from Europe, especially from Great Britain; interest payments in the form of foreign currencies constituted the new export of capital
  - ○ Britain was the leader in exporting capital
- **Britain** had tremendous export levels, building **railroads worldwide**
- An **international monetary system using the gold standard** was adopted by the "civilized" nations of the world
  - ○ Any currency could be turned to gold, and any gold could be turned to any currency
  - ○ The acceptance of the gold standard made trade extremely easy in the global marketplace
- **LONDON** was the center of the global economic and financial system
- Thus, an integrated world market was formed in which countries traded goods with one another
- This global system of trade was brought about by the Industrial Revolution. It served as a catalyst for making countries engage in specialization in order to maximize efficiency and profits within their nation
- **Invisible Exports:** The massive amount of imports paid for by "invisible exports": shipping and insurance services rendered to foreigners.
- International Money: Europe adopted the British gold standard by the 1870s, resulting high economic stability until 1914. Prices steadily fell until gold discoveries in the 1890s increased the supply.
- Debtors, including farmers and businessmen, were hurt, but creditors, the working classes and financiers, were helped.
- London bankers financed France's reparations in 1815 and even loaned money to Russia during the Crimean War.

- English "acceptance houses" paid English merchants for goods and collected through international banking channels. England was the bankers' banker, the insurers' insurer.

- World Market: Unity, Competition—and Insecurity: A true world market was created with goods, services, money, capital, and people who flowed easily across borders. Commodities were international, with supply and demand set wide.

- The system was precarious: a US grain surplus could ruin growers in Argentina. Factory owners faced brutal competition. Workingmen suffered if business was slow or jobs were eliminated by new machinery.

- Cycles of boom and depression began, with a long slide from 1873 to 1893. The economy was based on expansion and credit, and a collapse of confidence was deadly. Governments, to ensure against insecurities, used protective tariffs, social insurance, and welfare to an increasing degree.

- Laissez faire capitalism declined as unions and the socialist movement grew

- **International Money**:

- Europe adopted the British gold standard by the 1870s

- It resulted in high economic stability until 1914

- Prices steadily fell until gold discoveries in the 1890s increased the supply.

- **Changes in Big Business:**

- Many small businesses were replaced by large corporations

- Expensive machinery required more complex corporations

- Department stores developed and expanded

- Vertical & vertical integration

- In the steel industry, corporations bought out iron and coal mines and began producing steel, including both raw steel and manufactured.

- Buying out competitors served as a means of reducing competition: Increased corporate power, reduced fluctuations and increased stability.
   - US Steel (Carnegie)
   - Krupp in Germany
   - Schneider-Creusot in France
   - Vickers-Armstrong in Britain
      -

- **FRANCE:**
- The Republic of 1792 and 1848 was re-instituted after the defeat of France in 1870.
   - Free elections brought a monarchist majority
   - Parisians created the Commune
   - Patriotic and republican
   - Monarchists split
      - Orleanists and Bourbons

28

- **Troubles of the Third French Republic:**
    - The Republic was opposed by the upper classes, clergy, and army officers
    - Middle class was republican and had a parliamentary majority in 1879
    - General Boulanger, supported by radical republicans, dissatisfied workers, Bonapartists, and the monarchists
        - His program was to seek revenge on Germany through war
        - Dreyfus Affair (1894)
- **<u>Strength and Weakness of the Third French Republic</u>**
- The Republic stabilized France – it "domesticated democratic republicanism"
- Both the bourgeoisie and the peasants were comfortable, but were not ready for the transition to the modern industrial world
- Fell behind in industrial development because it didn't have entrepreneurial skills or stable government
    - Divided public opinion – many political parties and historical distrust of the executive authority
    - **Radical Socialists** (really Radical Republicans) represented small shopkeepers and farmers
    - Workers were angry because of the failure to establish a socialist republic - they distrusted government and politics (Republic had to face issue of labor, as well as other domestic and international problems).
- **<u>BRITISH CONSTITUTIONAL MONARCHY</u>**
- Self-government through Parliament
- Victorian Era (1837-1901): material progress, literary accomplishments, political stability
- Liberal **Gladstone** (industrial and commercial interests) and Conservative **Disraeli** (landed aristocracy) alternated in office; worked together to develop new policies
- Vote slowly expanded:
    - Reform Bill of 1833: include middle class
    - Second Reform Bill of 1867: include urban workers
    - Conservatives feared extending the vote further
    - The vote extended to rural workers in 1885
    - **In 1918 women over 30 can vote**
- Government is still run by upper classes: no salaries given to members of Parliament
- **<u>Political Changes after 1900</u>**
- Liberals pioneered state-supported public education (**Forester Education Act 1870**), secret ballot, legalizing labor unions, civil service exams, eliminating purchase of military commissions
- Conservatives led in labor legislation

- Rise of **Labour Party** led liberals to drop support of laissez-faire in favor of legislation for workers
- Liberals (**Asquith** and **David Lloyd George**): establish basic social welfare system, weakened strike restrictions, backed progressive income and inheritance tax
- **Parliament Act 1911**: removes the House of Lords' veto power, and pays the House of Commons
- Liberals become the party of labor, and conservatives the party of industry and landed wealth – but Labour would soon replace Liberals
- **The Irish Question**
- Ireland was incorporated into the UK to prevent pro-French sympathies in Ireland during French Revolution
- The Irish obstructed Parliament with grievances concerning absentee landlords and Anglican tithes
- The issue of home rule for Ireland split Gladstone's Liberals (conservatives didn't want the split)
    - Home rule granted in 1914
    - Ulstermen (Protestants in northern Ireland) didn't want to be part of a unified Ireland because they were outnumbered by Catholics
    - But the Catholics didn't want political division of Ireland, and Britain didn't want civil war
    - After much violence, Catholic Ireland receives dominion status and Ulster remains in UK with discontented Catholic minority
- **BISMARK and the German Empire**
    - Issues with the Catholic church: papacy tries to regain power
        - **Center Party**: defend Catholic interests
        - ***Kulturkampf*** ("battle for modern civilization"): restrictions on Catholic worship and education, expulsion of Jesuits, attacks on bishops
            - Much opposition, so he recinded policies
        - Next issue was with the **Social Democratic Party** (industrialism leads to stronger working class, which leads to socialism)
    - Bismarck attempted anti-socialist laws for 12 years, but social democrats weree still strong!
- **German Empire after 1890 – Wilhelm II**
- Wilhelm broke with Bismarck over issues of anti-socialist policies and foreign affairs
    - Wilhelm's rule: aggressive colonial, diplomatic, and naval path
    - Anti-socialist policies dropped, social security enhanced
    - Conciliated the masses

- - Issue of political democracy: would soon face a constitutional crisis
- **ITALY**
- Constitutional monarchy, but anticlerical
- Unstable majorities and shifting coalitions (*transformismo)*
- Increasing industry, better working classes, increased suffrage
- Unrest in cities because of illiteracy, inertia, and poverty
  - Anti-parliamentary ideology emerges
  - Nationalism, irrationalism, futuristic "nihilism"
- **AUSTRIA-HUNGARY**
  - - Constitutional parliament, but in reality Emperor Francis Joseph has control (he represses socialism)
    - Continued agitation of Slavic minorities, who are repressed by Magyars in Hungary
- **Europe in General**
- Europe is moving toward universal male suffrage, but little change for women until 1914
- Democracy is still advancing
  - Still many authoritarian monarchies
  - Only U.S., Britain, and France were true democracies
    - Social stability: more democratic and responsive to public opinion
    - Better conditions for middle and working classes: more able to participate in politics
    - Global economy, migration, military power (but opposition – socialism, critics of imperialism)

CHAPTER 5

EUROPEAN SOCIETY & CULTURE 1871-1914

- **<u>Trade Union Movement and Rise of British Labor</u>**
- After gaining the right to vote, members of the labor class now wanted to <u>improve their working conditions</u>.
    - Labor Unions had always been frowned upon (or deemed illegal) by governments.
    - **Some socialists wished to abolish capitalism**
    - Others wanted to bargain with them (labor unionists).
    - The prosperity of the 1850's favored the formation of unions, showing the emergence of **craft unions** as the first typical organizations.
    - There was an abandonment of "one big union".
    - Unions encouraged the specialization of goods.
- The British unions received recognition from the **Liberal Tories in 1825**, and explicit recognition by **Gladstone's liberal ministry in 1871**.
- French Unions were recognized by **Napoleon III in 1864**, then restrained temporarily by the **Paris Commune**, then **fully legalized in 1884.**
- In the 1880s, encouraged by the **Great London Dock Strike (1889)**, unions of unskilled workers began to form.
- **Industrial unionism**, or the joining into one union of all workers in one industry, regardless of occupation, began to take shape again.
    - There were many more unionists in Britain than the rest of Europe by 1900: 2 Million in Britain, 850,000 in Germany, and 250,000 in France.
    - British workers were actually far advanced in **trade unionism**. This slowed the formation of a labor party because workers were were so successful in forcing collective bargaining upon their employers..
    - In the 1880s, the few "Lib-Labs" (Liberal Democrats & Labour Party) in parliament were able to pass a Liberal Ticket for the working men.
        - It wasn't very socialistic and had grown fast due to a large measure in the desire to defend the unions as established.

- Finally, at the **turn of the 19th century**, the **British Labour Party** was formed through the joint efforts of trade union officials and middle-class intellectuals.

- The British Labour party was less socialistic than working-class parties on the continent. The party grew quickly because members wanted to be able to defend their respective unions as respectable institutions.

  o Unions were threatened by the **Taff Vale decision in 1901** which made unions **responsible for business losses incurred during a strike**.

    - By 1906, the Labour Party sent **29 members to Parliament**, so the Taffe Vale decision was <u>overruled</u>.

- **European Socialism after 1850**

- _European socialists and Marxists were divided on the tenets of socialism in many ways.

  o Marx, after spending 30 years in London, had scarcely mixed with labor unions.

  o In **1864** the first meeting of the **International Working Men's Association,** also known as the **First International**, took place in London.

    - At the meeting Marx took leadership, and used his position of power to publish his beliefs described in his *Das Capital*.

    - He made the Mazzinians feel unwelcome and denounced the Lassalleans for cooperating with Bismarck.

    - **Socialists are not supposed to cooperate with the governments, they're supposed to seize power from them.**

    - Biggest struggle at the conference was with **Bakunin (Russia)**; Bakunin believed the state was the cause of the common man's problems, as an anarchist, thought the state should be abolished

      - Marx HATED anarchism, as the state was a tool in class struggle; the true target for revolutionary action in favor of the proletariat was the capitalist economic system

    - Conference faded as the Paris Commune seemed to frighten followers after Marx called it a "dictatorship of the proletariat"

- 1875, **Gotha Conference**, Marxian and Lassallean socialists form the **German Social Democratic Party**

  o Belgian Socialist Party appears in 1879

  o France:

    - **Jules Guesde** - believed it impossible to emancipate workers by compromising

    - **Dr. Paul Brousse** - thought it would be possible for workers to arrive at socialism through parliamentary procedures

- **Jean Juares** - linked social reform to the French revolutionary tradition and the defense of republican institutions
- **1905: France forms a Socialist Party**
  - Great Britain: **H.M. Hyndman** founded a Social Democratic Federation (1881)
  - Russia: **Plekhanov and Axelrod** form Russian Social Democratic party (1883)
  - **In 1889 the Second International was formed by all the socialist parties.** Marx was dead by this time.

- <u>Revisionist and Revolutionary Socialism, 1880-1914</u>
  - _The mass of Marx's writing is known for its unyielding cooperation with competing socialists doctrines.
  - Marx failed to spread his ideas in Britain due to the fact that workers stood by their unions.
  - For the British, who were mostly **Fabians**, no class conflict was necessary. They believed that gradual measures would eventually bring about a socialist state and that improvements by local government would aid in this consummation.
  - The Fabians helped form the Labor party by joining with the unions.
  - Transformed into "parliamentary socialism"
  - Worker's goal was to get more for themselves; they would work for orderly legislation benefiting the workers of their own country only

- The proletariat was *not* getting poorer as Marx had predicted; real wages rose by 50% in industrialized countries from 1870 to 1900 (this was due to greater productivity of labor through mechanization, growing world economy, accumulation of capital wealth, fall in food prices and other resources)

- The **revisionists** held that class conflict might not be totally inevitable,
  - That capitalism might be gradually transformed in the workers interests, and that now workers had not only the vote, but their own political party: they could achieve their goals democratically.
  - **Revisionism**, led by **Jean Jaurès** and **Edouard Bernstein**, emerged: class conflict is not inevitable. In response, George Sorel created French syndicalism, with the idea of the rise of workers through a massive general strike.
  - The German **Karl Kautsky** attacked revisionism as petit bourgeois compromise (i.e., "opportunism"). The conflict came in London in 1903, where Lenin demanded the end of revisionism. Lenin termed his party the Bolsheviks (majority), and the revisionists as the Mensheviks (minority)

- Trade Unionism = **Syndicalism**
- <u>Women's Rights</u>
- The campaign for women's rights became more organized and widespread during the late 19th century.

- o Women had been receiving **less pay than men**, and also faced numerous **restrictions on their rights to own property**, participate in **political meetings**, **vote** in elections, and **attend universities**.
  - o **Women's groups in Europe** emphasized legal and social reforms rather than just voting rights, while those in Britain and the US devoted their campaign to suffrage.
  - o American women such as **Elizabeth Cady Stanton** and **Susan B. Anthony** joined with the European feminists to establish the **International Council of Women in 1888.**
  - o Some feminists worked to make birth control more available while others wished to improve their working conditions.
  - o Organizations like the **National American Woman Suffrage Association (NAWSA; USA)** and the **Women's Social and Political Union (Britain)** sponsored petitions, mass meetings, and protests that demanded equal voting rights in all elections.
- In Britain, women became very militant under the leadership of **Emmeline Pankhurst.**
  - o Pankhurst led a radical wing of suffragettes into a campaign of violent protests, breaking windows, mailboxes, and property.
  - o When arrested, they went on hunger strikes.
  - o Eventually, in 1918, women over the age of 30 were given the right to vote.
  - o Germany, the US, and other western nations saw suffrage for women after World War One.
  - o The movements for complete equality and more rights for women would not be completed until later in the twentieth century.
- The late 19th century saw an emphasis of biology and the life sciences.
- **Gregor Mendel,** an Austrian monk, experimented with crossbreeding of garden peas. He discovered the principle of heredity.
- **Charles Darwin published *Origin of the Species* in <u>1859</u>,** stamping evolution with the seal of science.
  - o Darwin said was that all species have evolved over time. Some species in the "struggle for existence" inherit qualities that allow for the "survival of the fittest" through "natural selection."
  - o He published **The Descent of Man** in <u>1871</u>, applying the same hypothesis to human beings.
  - o **"Survival of the Fittest":** organisms all vary in one small way or another. Some organisms have variations that are beneficial and provide advantages in survival.
    - Terms used by Darwin, (but not exactly *first* used by Darwin): "Struggle for existence", "survival of the fittest", "Natural selection", "most favored races".
  - o His ideas created a massive outcry from the public, and he (and the theory of evolution) was defended by Thomas Huxley.

- o There was a fear that all grounds of human dignity, morality, and religion would collapse because humans "came from monkeys".
    - The literal interpretation in the chapter of Genesis (in the Bible) was undermined by evolution.
- o The elimination of the weak is only natural. Literally.
- o Darwinism merged with the Toughness of Mind, or *Realpolitik.*
- o Darwin's theory sparked severe reactions from the church. It was also used to rationalize imperialism of European forces during the 1880's in Africa, used to distinguish certain races as more superior than others: **Social Darwinism**.
    - Some people are naturally superior to others (whites to blacks, Germans to Slavs, Non-Jews to Jews, Middle/Upper classes compared to the lower classes).
    - Big businesses should to take over smaller businesses.
    - Some states were bound to rise over others.
    - War was morally a fine thing.
    - Darwin expressed a world without need of God.

- **Anthropology and sociology** were established to explain behavior. Anthropology studied races to find the "superior" in inheritance and survival value
- Anthropologists showed that no culture was superior, that all were adaptations to environment
- Anthropology seemed to undermine traditional religious beliefs
- Psychology was equally upsetting
  o Pavlov's work with conditioning: the idea that much behavior was based on conditioned responses.
- o **Freud founded psychoanalysis**: the study of causes of current behavior and the power of the subconscious.
- **Physics –**
  o Becquerel discovered that uranium emitted particles or rays of energy
  o J. J. Thompson and Rutherford showed that atoms were complex and that some were "radioactive"
  o Max Planck showed that energy was emitted or absorbed in units called quanta
  o Niels Bohr postulated that an atom with a nucleus of protons was surrounded by electrons
  o **Einstein** showed that matter was convertible into energy and denied the absolute character of time, space, and motion in his theory of relativity. His unified field theory brought a new view of the universe, challenging Euclid and Newton

Philosophy

- **Friedrich Nietzsche** believed that from mankind would emerge the Superman who would lead and dominate the masses. He viewed Christian ideals (humility, patience, love, hope) as a slave morality

- Scriptural critics, analyzed the Bible for inconsistencies and explaining away miracles as myth.

- People turned to materialistic progress rather than spiritual values

- **The Churches and the Modern Age**

- **Lateran Treaty 1929**: unified Italy

  o The Pope lost temporal powers, but gained independence from national or secular authority

- **Leo XIII** (revival of medieval philosophy) – *de Rerum Novarum* ("of modern things"): criticized capitalism for poverty, insecurity, degradation of working classes; proclaimed need for social justice (socialism could be Christian, but denounced Marxism for its materialism and irreligion).

- **Jewish Emancipation**

- Reform Judaism is counterpart to Christian modernism

- Liberalism brought citizenship to Jews and assimilation, but this was slowed by **anti-Semitism** (from Jewish competition, fear of Jewish Marxists, and growing ethnic nationalism)

- This led many Jews to **Zionism**, a political movement begun by **Theodore Herzl** in 1897, which called for a national home for the Jews in Palestine.

- **WANING OF CLASSICAL LIBERALISM**

- Basics of classical liberalism:

  o Stressed liberty of the individual

  o Stressed education and opposed imposition of force on individual because believed people could discuss differences and produce progress through peaceable compromise

  o Wanted constitutional governments: limited power, chosen representatives

  o Favored will of majority, but minorities should be respected because individuals changed opinions of others

  o Favored universal male suffrage, laissez-faire, international economic system, toleration

- But there were hardships of a free/market economy:

  o **Friedrich List**: *National System of a Political Economy* 1840: only industrialized Britain would benefit from free trade – agrarian countries would not

  o Decline of free trade to protect agricultural interests: demands for protective tariffs

  o **Economic nationalism** (subordinate economic activities to political ends) led to imperialism and competition for markets (especially between Germany, U.S., and Japan)

  o Workers form unions as industries form monopolies: this organized labor and big business undermines individual competition of classical liberalism

- o **Social service state** develops: assumes responsibility for social and economic welfare of the masses – protects the individual!
- o New Liberals (Teddy Roosevelt, David Lloyd George) accept a major role for government
- o Organized labor, socialist parties, universal male suffrage, and sensitivity to social distress lead to political intervention in economies: governments weaken big business and strengthen the worker (the aim is to reestablish economic competition and individualism).
- o *Now, people begin to fear an overly centralized government*
  - ▪ Belief in **anti-intellectualism**: can't settle matters by discussion because everyone is already prior conditioned
  - ▪ Philosophy of "realism": faith in value of struggle and tough-minded rejection of ideals:
    - Darwin and Freud stress the irrational and conflict
    - Marx – class warfare
    - Nietzsche – manly virtues
    - Social Darwinists – glorified success
    - Sorel (*Reflections on Violence* 1908): all violence is beneficial. Belief in "myth" of a future general strike to keep people excited, even though he never thought it would really happen – this leads to fascism.
    - Even in England (homeland of liberalism), classical liberalism declines: tariffs, Labour Party solidarity, Liberals abandon laissez faire, Irish resistance by force, violence of suffragettes
- But liberalism persists!
  - o Tariffs enacted, but still have world trade
  - o Nationalism, but not totalitarianism
  - o Protection of minorities and Jews
  - o Still humanitarian trade, even though no laissez faire
  - o Social democrats were revisionists, and did not believe in a social catastrophe
  - o Governments glorified war, but people and other organizations still tried to prevent it
  - o Skepticism, but still faith in progress

NOTE: At this point Europe has gone through a long period without a major war, but now the major nation-states are seeking geopolitical and economic advantages. War is inevitable.

CHAPTER 6

EUROPEAN GEOPOLITICAL SUPREMACY 1871-1914

IMPERIALISM: ITS NATURE AND CAUSES

- **The New Imperialism**
- **World civilization develops (increasing gap between modern and traditional)**
  - All nations participate in a world economy, but industry only helps the western countries
  - "Backwards" countries are harmed by modern economic and social changes: they do not adapt well to the new situation (example: Africa)
- Europeans seem very powerful to the rest of the world because they are so united (because of the nationalist movements). The non-European powers (except Japan) were in decay: ex: Ottoman empire, Russia
- **European ("western") countries move into backwards countries to gain wealth – neomercantilism**
- Replacing the old imperialism (marine and mercantile), new imperialism develops in late 19C because European powers want newer and greater quantities of goods
- The neomercantilists invest capital into these backward countries. Obtain raw materials from colonies, and sell manufactured goods back to them.
- Native workers are exploited
- Imperialists become much more involved financially and politically (example: India).
- **Colonies become equated with power**
- Because imperialists are so economically entwined with these countries, they want them to remain under their control
- Creation of colonies, protectorates (India and Dutch East Indies), and spheres of influence (China and Persia)
- Imperialist countries use their industrial power and military technology to control their territories
- **Territorial domination results because Europeans needed more production and a greater quantity of goods** to maintain a higher standard of living.

40

- Exploited, natives form an unhappy working class
- Territorial domination in:
  - Mexico: US cotton growers expand plantation culture, but want to obey US laws. This leads to Mexican-American War 1845
  - Persia (Afghanistan) – conflict between British (builds a telegraph line and discovers oil fields) and Russia: referred to as "The Great Game". By 1907, it is carved into spheres of influence
  - China: trades opium with the west, but this leads to Opium War. Under Treaty of Nanking, China is forced to open treaty ports: leads to spheres of influence
- Colonies: direct rule
  - Spain: Cuba: first "concentration" camps under General Weyler
  - US: Puerto Rico and the Philippines after the Spanish-American War 1898
  - India, before Sepoy Revolt 1857
- Typically, once backwards countries start to rebel, imperialist powers tighten their hold on them
- Protectorates: rule through the local governments
  - **Platt Amendment**: US controls Cuba (geopolitics!)
  - **Roosevelt Corollary:** allows US to be the police force. Saves Latin American countries from European powers, but not from US!
  - **India** (after Sepoy) and Dutch East Indies: model forms! (culture system)
  - **Egypt**: Britain wants to control Suez
  - **Africa** (International Congo Association – 1878)
- Countries are technically independent (Persia and China, see above) as protectorates obtained under a "natural" sphere of influence
- **Additional Incentives for Imperialism as a Crusade**
- **Economic**:
  - Maintain higher European standard of living
  - Increasing trade with other parts of the world – leads to exploiting the colonies or territories for their natural resources
  - Money invested in "backward" countries brought a higher rate of return than if invested in more industrialized ones
    - Cheap labor
    - Heavy and unsatisfied demand for non-European products
  - Most exported capital was British-owned
  - The demand for imports was needed to sustain the European population, and the demand for such imports made investment in colonies financially profitable
  - Surplus European population can migrate to these places

- **Non-economic**:
  - Social Darwinism - other people are inferior to Europeans
    - White Man's Burden: the belief that it was the civilized world's duty to help the backwards countries
  - Colonies = power
  - Chances of history made the European the leading civilization, and although just for the present, Europeans must keep guardianship over the others
  - Also: Christian missionaries, scientific expeditions, traveling for wealthy people
- **Socialist critiques**:
  - Joseph Chamberlain: believed in municipal socialism (beginning the idea of a commonwealth)
    - Urged the dominions of Britain to charge a lower duty on British products than on products from other countries
    - Proposed that Britain adopt a protective tariff
    - Wanted to **bind the empire by economic bonds, making a tariff union, or system of "imperial preference"**
      - Although he died in 1914, after WW1 his ideas were adopted
  - **Hobson and Lenin *(Imperialism, the Highest Stage of World Capitalism*)**: Blamed imperialism on capitalist need to invest surplus capital – of more income went to workers, there would be no surplus and therefore no need for imperialism
    - Since the working class would have more purchasing power, it would be less necessary to search endlessly for new markets outside the country
- **THE AMERICAS**
- **Looking back**
- Breakup of Spanish and Portuguese empires at the start of the 19th century left land unsettled
- The people of this unsettled land were Indian, Mestizo or European
- Brazil became independent of Portugal in 1822 but was a monarchy until 1889 when it became a republic
- Spanish empire, disappearance of royal rule were left as flaccid republics, constantly having border disputes
- Congress of Vienna - thought of returning these republics to Spain, but 1823 Monroe Doctrine from US opposed it
- **The United States and Mexico**
- After becoming independent of Spain, Mexico stretched to the Mississippi and the Rockies

- Mexican republic forbid slavery
  - However, land settlers from the West poured into Mexico with their slaves to grow cotton to meet increasing European demand
- Texas
  - Newcomers in Mexico proclaim their own republic
  - 1845-US annexed Texas
  - Caused Mexican-American War
    - Mexico lost, gave up Texas to California coast, losing half of their territory to their aggressive neighbor
    - US argued they were better off than Mexico to "civilize" the region
- Mexico had contracted large loans on exorbitant terms, so European lenders estimated Mexican credit to be unstable
- Benito Juarez
  - Pure-blooded Indian
  - Liberal
  - Repudiated the loans causing European bondholders to demand payment
- US was caught up in the Civil War at the time
- Great Britain, France, Spain send military forces to Veracruz
  - **Britain**
    - Seized customs houses in Mexico and use revenue to pay of debt
    - Wanted repayment, and had no territorial ambitions
  - **France**
    - Wants to control Mexico so that from there could flow French capital and exports
    - Had territorial ambitions
    - Mexican empire with Archduke Maximilian (Austria) as emperor
  - Britain and Spain withdraw their forces
  - France takes over, but Napoleon decided the whole attempt to conquer Mexico was too expensive
  - France thought the US would collapse during the Civil War. When it didn't, France left Mexico.
  - Juarez back in power!
- **Monroe Doctrine (1820)** was an effective barrier to European territorial ambitions. Still, Latin America never became subject to American imperialism as completely as Asia and Africa.
- In 1903 the US facilitated a revolution in Panama against Columbia and then guaranteed the Panamanian independence: all to get the Panama Canal built. The US leases the canal for 99 years.

- In 1898, US sentiment backed a **Cuban revolution against Spain**. U.S. economic and political self-interest was also important: US citizens had $50 million invested, needed Cuban sugar, and had strategic interests. Spain was portrayed as barbaric and brutal in the US "yellow press" (not entirely incorrect considering General Weyler's conduct) and the loss of the Maine brought war.

- In the resulting peace treaty, the US took Puerto Rico and the Philippines, and Cuba was made a protectorate by means of the **Platt Amendment**.

- During the same time Teddy Roosevelt advanced the Roosevelt Corollary to the Monroe Doctrine: instability within a nation allows intervention to prevent problems. The US was to intervene constantly in Central America/Caribbean until 1932 - Dollar Diplomacy.

- **Hawaii**

- The story of Hawaii is typical of American intervention and expansionism: By 1840, US sailors, whalers, missionaries and merchants were established in the island. Hawaii became a protectorate in 1875 to gain access to Pearl Harbor and trade privileges. US capital was invested heavily in sugar and pineapple (brought from Mexico by the Doles, missionaries). In 1891 Queen Liliuokalani tried to limit Western penetration. She was overthrown by Americans living on the island.

- Rudyard Kipling: "White Man's Burden"; members of the white race are superior and have the responsibility of conquering other races and making them civilized (paternalism)

    - **Puerto Rico** was annexed in 1898

    - **Foraker Act**: 1900: Puerto Rico is a US colony, The president of the US would approve governor for PR. The upper house has to be appointed by the president and the lower house is appointed by the PRs.

    - **James Act** (1917): Puerto Ricans are made US citizens

- Theodore Roosevelt said "uncivilized nations that show weakness or misbehavior may require intervention from a civilized nation."

- **The Ottoman Empire** was viewed as the "sick man of Europe".

- The main reason dissolution was because the Ottomans were not keen on the "westernization" of their country; they felt that maintaining practices that had kept them alive for hundreds of years should be continued.

    - Since the Ottoman Empire **lost Hungary in 1699**, the Empire was headed towards decline.

    - The **Crimean War** also negatively affected the Ottomans, even though they were on the winning side. Exposing their military and political weakness, the war pointed out that the country **needed to be better organized**.

        - The outcome of the war was taken to prove the superiority of the political systems of England and France.

- Turkish reformers wished to remodel on Western lines.

- o Although the Ottomans attempted to reform military and political systems between 1856 and 1876, the conservative country was not entirely compliant.
  - Newspapers founded
  - National Turkish revival of history
  - **Abdul Aziz =** first sultan to visit Europe
  - However, few Turks had the skill or experience to reform Turkey
- o Reformist minister **Midhat Pasha** deposed Aziz in 1876, put **Abdul Hamid II** in power
  - Produced a new constitution in 1876, declared Ottoman empire indivisible and promised liberty and freedom
  - First Turkish parliament met in 1877, addressed ideas of reform
- o The ruler, **Abdul Hamid**, was ACTUALLY anti-reformist
  - He got rid of Pasha, the parliament and threw away the constitution
  - Caused Young Turks, the educated young reformists, to seek exile in Europe
  - Responded to nationalist uprisings brutally (Bulgarian massacre of 1876, Armenian massacre of 1894); shocked Europeans who were not used to such violence
  - Not open to the educational systems of the west; viewed the chemistry textbooks printed in the United States as seditious because the symbols used might be a secret message.
  - He believed that abandonment from traditional Ottoman ways would lead to destruction of the Empire.
  - The Young Turks sought to overthrow him
- **Russo-Turkish War** brought about dissolution of the Ottomans
  - o Pan-Slavism favored the Russians
  - o Insurrection broke out, Russians swept in as the Ottoman empire collapsed before the Russians
  - o **Treaty of San Stefano (1878)**
    - Ceded to Russia **Batum and Kars**
    - Full independence to **Serbia and Romania**
    - Promised reforms in **Bosnia**
    - Granted autonomy to **Bulgaria**
  - o **Russian jingoism** - extreme patriotism in the form of aggressive foreign policy
- European imperialists in the late 1800s were also responsible for the dissolution of the Ottoman Empire.
  - o The French took Algeria and Tunisia from the Turks in 1830

- o The Italians took Libya in 1912
- o England took Egypt in 1882
- o Austria took the northern part of the empire. Because of European powers, the Ottoman Empire was reduced to Turkey, a weak state

- **Division of Africa**
- Positive aspects for the African colonized peoples were limited.
    - o One of these was the fact that a very limited number of Africans were offered a western education
- Negative aspects
    - o The imperialist process was good for the European powers, at the expense of African peoples.
        - Raw materials from colonies boosted the European economies and added to their power and influence.
    - o The literacy rates were low and infant mortality rates were very high in Africa and other colonized countries.
    - o Africa was controlled by European powers who never took the quality of life of African natives into consideration, their only concern was for personal gain.
    - o Even after African territories gained independence, the governments were unstable, and war broke out all over the continent. The new African republics were corrupt.
- The most long-lasting effect was the **arbitrary political boundaries** which European monarchies established, and which ignored the previous tribal system.
    - o Most of these boundaries are still here today, and have been one of the major causes for African civil wars and conflicts.
- Otto von Bismarck thought that African colonies were an absurdity, and called for another **conference in Berlin in 1885:** this time to submit the African question to **international regulation.**
    - o Most European states as well as the US attended the conference.
    - o The Berlin Conference had two goals: to set up territories of the Congo Association as an international states, under international auspices and restrictions; and to draft a code governing the way in which European powers wishing to acquire African territory should proceed.
- Indirect Rule: Tribal Chiefs given autonomy and work for imperialists
- There was still conflict on the African continent.
    - o **Fashoda Crisis:** English and the French came extremely close to war over territories along the Nile River.
    - o Because the English had a larger army and navy, the French stepped down and allowed the English to seize most of Eastern Africa.

- o In March 1899, the French and British agreed that the source of the Nile and the Congo rivers should mark the frontier between their spheres of influence.
- o In the **Boer War (1899 - 1902)** between the Afrikaans and the British over territory in South Africa. The discovery of gold and diamonds in the Boer Republics brought a great rush of Europeans
    - Netherlands did not support the war as Afrikaners were of Dutch descent. The international relations of the time were awful, and this led to tensions that erupted in the First World War.

- **Russo-Turkish War of 1877-78:**
- Russia still dreamed of capturing Istanbul and the vital straits. They supported Slavic nationalist movements, leading to insurrections in Bosnia and Bulgaria.
- The result was the (6th) Russo-Turkish War. The Russians forced the Turks to accept the Treaty of San Stefano (1877), giving them the Caucasus territories and bringing varying degrees of autonomy to Rumania, Serbia, Bulgaria, and Bosnia.
- Britain, nervous over Suez, called for war in a jingoistic clamor. To avert problems which might aid France to gain allies, Bismarck entered as "honest broker" and called the...

- **Congress of Berlin:**
- Russia kept the **trans-Caucasus region** (Armenia, Azerbaijan); Serbia, Rumania, Montenegro were independent; Bulgaria was nominally independent under the Ottoman Empire; Bosnia was occupied and administered by Austria.
- Britain got **Cyprus**, France expanded into **Tunisia**, and Italy was promised **Albania**. Italy had a "great appetite but poor teeth", as Bismarck noted.
- Germany took no territory, but it had earned Turkish good will; German capital was exported, as in the case of the Berlin to Bagdad railroad.
- Egypt, meanwhile, moved to modernize. **Railroads** were built and cotton exports increased hugely, 1861-1865. Mismanagement and luxury spending by the elite brought debt, and increased Western influence--bringing nationalistic, anti-Western feeling and riots--which Britain used as an excuse to move in, with Egypt as a protectorate.
- Upset, the French began to expand, moving from Algeria into Tunisia and Morocco, upsetting the British and the Germans. The"Young Turks" gained control of the Ottoman government in 1908 and returned to the constitution of 1876.
- Bulgaria declared its independence and Austria annexed Bosnia; Italy took Libya by force in 1911-12. The Balkan wars of 1912-13 cost Turkey virtually all of its European territory. In 1914, Russia declared war on Turkey, which joined Germany in World War I. (Modern Turkey emerged in its present form in 1919.)

- **The Partition of Africa**
- The Opening of Africa: Africa was the romanticized "**Dark Continent**" of gold and slaves, and missionaries like **David Livingstone. H. M. Stanley** went to Africa on a journalistic junket to "find" Livingstone--who was not "lost."

- Stanley found Dr. Livingstone, but more importantly, he realized the imperialistic value of Africa. Backed by Leopold of Belgium and financiers, he founded the International Congo Association (1878) to exploit the region.

- He concluded 500 "treaties" with tribal chiefs, gaining vast areas for small outlays from peoples who had no concept of property in the Western sense. Karl Peters in East Africa, Brazza in the West, did the same for Germany and France.

- Portugal, too, began to expand its coastal holds deep inland. The Berlin Congress of 1885 called for open trade, protection of native rights, and no slavery, but there was no enforcement machinery. The reality was the incredible brutalization of the people of the Congo to squeeze out maximum profits. Nowhere was imperialism worse.

- Ethiopia proved able to defend itself, defeating the Italians at Adowa in 1895.

- Britain had territories in both the South and north, which it hoped to be able to unite. The British were defeated in Sudan in 1885.

- **The establishment of "rules"**

- Led to a scramble for territory in the interior--and by 1900 all of Africa except Liberia and Ethiopia were claimed.

- Chiefs rarely had power to grant any sort of rights, so the Europeans built up the chief's power in order to gain control. They then ruled through these chiefs.

- The main problem was always labor, since the African lacked a sense of money or possessions and regarded continuous labor as the lot of women.

- The result was forced labor--either semi-slavery or by levying a money tax or reducing native lands to the point that survival required work. Native societies were uprooted, and the individual was left alone, with nothing to replace the tribe or village.

- The westernized class grew--chiefs, Christian priests, clerks. Many went to western universities, where they came to resent paternalism and exploitation. African nationalism had its genesis in these young people.

- **India**

- **Sepoy Revolt of 1857:** caused by the British attitude to caste and Muslim fundamentalism

- The main result was the closing of the British East India Company rule and the last Moguls, replacing them with both direct British rule and rule through Indian principalities

- British industry wiped out India's textiles, promoted exports of cotton, tea, jute, indigo, wheat

- A major rail system was built to facilitate trade

- English was made the language of rule
    - Nationalism spread
    - anti-British
    - pro-Hindu or pro-Muslim.

- **Imperialism in Asia: China and the West**

48

- **China**
- The **modern and unfavorable phase** of Chinese relations with the West was **opened** by the opium trade, eventually leading to **Opium War of 1839-1841**:
- The Europeans wanted Chinese products, but the Chinese had no interest in buying European goods.
    - The Europeans forcefully entered China through the **Treaty of Nanking (1842)** and the **Treaties of Tientsin (1857)**, whose terms were soon duplicated in still other treaties signed by China with other European powers and with the United States.
    - Europeans opened **"treaty ports"**: in these cities Europeans were allowed to make settlements of their own, immune to Chinese law *(much like Americans in Mexico under President Hayes)*
    - China became a free trade market for European goods (no import duty over 5%)
    - Early set up for the American **Open Door Policy**
    - European governments defended Manchu (Qing) government from internal opposition because they relied on it to promote their own interests
- The **"Open Door Policy"** was announced by the United States, fearing that China might soon be parceled out into exclusive spheres.
    - The idea of the Open Door was that China should remain territorially intact and independent.
    - Powers having special influences should maintain the 5 percent Chinese tariff and allow businessmen of all nations to trade without discrimination.
    - The British supported the Open Door policy as a means of discouraging actual annexations by Japan or Russia.
    - **Boxer Rebellion 1899**: occurred because of increasing nationalist movement against outsiders.
    - Eventually, nationalism will grow even more, with the National People's Party
- **Japan**
- Japan lost little time in developing imperialistic tendencies.
    - An expansionist party already looked to the Chinese mainland and to the South.
    - Japanese imperialism first revealed itself to the world in 1894, when Japan went to war with China over disputes in Korea (**Sino-Japanese War**)
        - The Japanese won, equipped as they were with modern weapons, training, and organization.
        - T hey obliged the Chinese to sign the **treaty of Shimonoseki in 1895,** by which **China ceded Formosa and the Liaotung**

peninsula to Japan and **recognized Korea as an independent state.**

- The Liaotung was a tongue of land reaching down from Manchuria to the sea.

  - This soon led to the **Russo-Japanese War**

    - Causes Russia to shift attention to the west (Balkans and Persia)

    - Weakened Russia, led to takeover by the Bolsheviks

    - News of Japan's victory shocked the world; they finally noticed that a non-European country might compete militarily/economically

      o Inspires other small nations with hope that they too may one day be free and powerful like Japan; caused revolts in Asia

- **Russo-Japanese War and its Consequences**
- _Russia and Japan opposed each other's intrigues in Manchuria and Korea.

  o The Japanese felt a need for supplying their new factories with raw materials and markets on the Asian mainland, for employment for their newly westernized army and navy, and for recognized status as a Great Power in the Western sense.

  o The Russian government needed an atmosphere of crisis and expansion to stifle criticism of the Tsar at home; it could not abide the presence of a strong power directly on its East Asian frontier, it could use Manchuria and Korea to strengthen the exposed outpost of Vladivostok, which was somewhat squeezed against the sea and landlocked by Japanese waters.

- Japan had just as much expansionist ambition as Russia, yet Japan was a more organized nation (militarily and politically).

  o In the war (fought in 1895), the Japanese saw the fruits of their success against China greedily enjoyed by their Russian rival.

  o In 1902 Japan signed a military alliance with Great Britain.

  o We have seen how the British were alarmed by their diplomatic isolation after Fashoda and the Boer War, and for how many years they had been expecting to have trouble with Russia. Here it begins!

    - The Anglo-Japanese alliance lasted for 20 years.

    - War broke out in 1904 and Japan swiftly destroyed the Russian fleet, to the surprise of European powers.

- The Russo-Japanese war was the first war between Great Powers since 1870.

  o It was the first war fought under conditions of developed industrialism.

  o It was the first actual war between westernized powers to be caused by competition in the exploitation of undeveloped countries.

- Most significant of all, it was the first time that a nation of nonwhite people had defeated a nation of white people in modern times.
- Asians had shown that they could learn to play, in less than half a century, the game of Europeans.

- The Japanese victory set off long chains of repercussions in at least 3 different directions:
  - First the Russian Government shifted its attention back to Europe, where it resumed an active role in the affairs of the Balkans.
    - This contributed to a series of international crises in Europe, in which the result was the First World War.
  - Second, the Tsarist government was weakened by the war, both in prestige and in actual military strength.
    - Opinion in Russia was so disgusted at the clumsiness and incompetency with which the war had been handled, that the various anti-Tsarist underground movements were able to surface, producing the Russian revolution of 1905.
    - This was a prelude to the **Great Russian Revolution** twelve years later, from which Soviet communism was the outcome.
  - Third, news of Japan's victory over Russia electrified those who heard of it throughout the non-European world.
    - The fact that Japan itself was an imperialist power was overlooked in the excited realization that the Japanese were not a European power.
    - Only half a century ago, the Japan had been "backward", defenseless, bombarded, and dominated by the Europeans.

- The implications were clear: leaders around the world concluded that bringing Western science into their countries and industry was needed for success.
  - This must be done by getting rid of the control by Europeans, supervising the industrialization & modernization themselves.
  - This ideology spurred nationalist revolutions all over the world:
    - Persia in 1905
    - Turkey in 1908
    - China in 1911
  - The self-assertion of Asians was to grow in intensity after WWI

CHAPTER 7

WORLD WAR I

Triple Alliance versus Triple Entente

- Many had long thought that a united Germany would revolutionize Europe
  - By 1900, Germany produced more steel than FR and GB combined
  - Germans felt they deserved "their place in the sun"
  - Bismarck followed a policy of peace until his retirement in 1890
  - Looked with satisfaction on French colonial expansion
  - 1879: forms alliance with Austria-Hungary; 1882: forms alliance with Italy
    - **TRIPLE ALLIANCE is formed!**
- **Triple Alliance**
  - Germany + Austria-Hungary + Italy
  - If any member became involved in war, they would help each other out
    - Bismarck signed reinsurance treaty with Russia, but Austria opposed Russia, so the alliance failed
    - France jumps at the chance to form an alliance with Russia (**Franco-Russian Alliance of 1894**)
    - Anti-British sentiments lingered in Europe post-Fashoda crisis and Boer War
    - **"Splendid isolation"**-Britain had been going their own way, didn't want dependence on an alliance
    - **1898**-Germany builds navy
- **Naval race**
  - **British sea power** had always been dominant
  - **Mahan:** sea power was the source of Britain's greatness. Germans avidly read his books
- Germany insisted on having a navy to protect colonies, secure foreign trade, and to project power and prestige
- British emerge from isolation in 1902; form alliance with Japan

- *Entente cordiale* - France and Britain set aside their differences (1904), as well as their problems with Russia for fear of German power
- **Triple Entente (the Allies)**- France + Britain + Russia
- Crises in Morocco
  - **French** were taking over Morocco
  - **Kaiser William II** made speech in favor of Moroccan independence in 1905
  - It was in effect an attempt to keep France out of Morocco
    - Germans demanded and obtained an international conference at Algeciras; conference supported French claims in Morocco (1906)
    - FR and GB become even stronger
  - Second Morocco Crisis (1911)
    - Panther, German gunboat, gets to Agadir to "protect German interests"
    - Germany agreed to leave if they got the French Congo (they ended up just get a few minor concessions)
  - Crises in the Balkans
    - Serbs and Bosnians- (side with Russia) Cyrillic writing, Eastern orthodox
    - Croats and Slovenes (side with western Europe) Roman writing, Roman Catholic religion
    - Slav revivalist movements promotes creation of an independent state
    - Meant that an element of Austro-Hungarian empire (mainly Croats and Slovenes) want to join Serbia
      - Young Turks have a revolution, oblige sultan to restore liberal constitution of 1876
        - Russia turned to get involved in the Balkans after being defeated by Japan
  - **Conference at Buchlau (1908)**
    - Russian foreign minister - Isvolsky
    - Austrian foreign minister - von Aehrenthal
    - Agree to have Russia favor annexation of Bosnia to Austria and Austria would support opening of straits to Russian warships
    - However, Austria, without waiting for a conference, proclaimed annexation of Bosnia
    - This angered the Serbs who had planned to annex Bosnia!
    - Bulgaria became independent
    - Crete united with Greece

- Austrian influence grew in the Balkans
- Southern slavic nationalism grew
- Italy declares war on Turkey in 1911; Bulgaria, Serbia and Greece side with Turkey
  - Turkey lost
- The Sarajevo Crisis and the Outbreak of War
  - Assassination!
  - Bosnian revolutionary (member of the Black Hand) assassinated Archduke Francis Ferdinand
  - Ferdinand was known to favor political transformation of Austria-Hungary which may have given greater equality to the Slavs
  - Possible reason he was killed: he could make the system work for all enemies of the revolutionaries
  - Austrian government was determined to end South Slavic separatism, that was Germans issue 'blank check" to encourage Austrians to be firm
  - Serbs count on Russian support, Russians count on French support; French was scared of war with Germany, so they issued blank check to Russia
  - Austria declared war on Serbia, Russia mobilized, Austria declared war on Russia
  - Evasiveness of British policy on the war contributed to its cause (had they immediately gotten involved Germany may have backed down
  - Germany violated Belgian neutrality by invading them in order to invade France
- England sees its time to declare war!
  - Russia and Austria were tottering empires; Tsarist regime suffered from revolutionary fervor, Habsburgs had to deal with chronic nationalism
  - Treat of Brest-Litovsk pulls Russia out of the war
  - German empire faced internal crisis
  - Social Democrats become majority in Reichstag in 1912
  - However, govt. didn't recognize the power of the Reichstag so they continued being warlike.
- Policy was determined by the upper classes who wanted navy and army (strong business interests)
- Industrial countries now became vulnerable to a loss in raw materials and sales of manufactured goods
  - Imperialism driven
  - Quest to build alliances

- **The Armed Stalemate**
  - The War on the Land
    - Most people expected a short war, but it lasted through four years of appalling losses.
    - Germany launched its attack with 78 divisions against about the same Allied strength; a surprisingly rapid Russian offensive forced reduced strength; overextended by their rapid surge, the Germans were slowed and then stopped by the counter-attack called the Battle of the Marne.
    - The Russians were defeated in the East and the whole Western front turned into trench warfare, dominated by artillery and the machine gun.
    - The second year of the war brought Russian successes against Austria and the Allied attempt to punch through the Dardanelles to supply Russia--the Gallipoli campaign.
    - The third year was characterize by the two great battles of attrition, Verdun (launched by Germany) and the Somme (launched by Britain). Artillery was built up on a massive scale and losses were immense, with no real gains.
    - Poison gas was introduced at Verdun, and the tank at the Somme--neither with intelligence or success.
  - The War at Sea
    - Both sides blockaded the other, violating a 1909 agreement on contraband/non-contraband trading.
    - Neutrals were kept out of German ports, and the US called for "freedom of the seas."
    - Germany countered by using submarines, declaring a war zone around Britain in February of 1915. The sinking of the Lusitania in May (it carried both contraband and 1200 passengers) shocked the US and Germany, concerned about US entry, backed down.
    - The only major sea battle was the Battle of Jutland, after which German surface ships were kept bottled up.
  - Diplomatic Maneuvers and Secret Agreements
    - The Ottoman Empire, traditional rival of Russia, quickly joined Germany; Bulgaria, being anti-Serb, joined the Central Powers in 1915.
    - Italy bargained with both sides; promised the Trentino, Trieste, and south Tyrol ("Italia Irridenta") in a secret treaty, Italy joined the Allies--in spite of divided public opinion.
    - The Allies made plans to divide up the Ottoman spoils: Russia (Armenia, the Bosporus), Britain (Iraq); and France (Syria).
    - Germany worked to stir up subject nationalities like the Poles and Ukrainians, talked of "holy war" with Muslims, worked with Irish

Republicans, and sent the Zimmerman Note to Mexico to gain Mexico's support if the US ever joined the war.

- German war aims remained decidedly expansionistic.

o Slavic and Arab hopes for independence

- The Allies worked on Slavic and Arab hopes for independence (with the work of T. E. Lawrence, "Lawrence of Arabia"), and Lord Balfour made promises concerning a Jewish homeland in Palestine.
- The Japanese entered the war to gain German colonies in the Pacific and to move further into both Manchuria and North China.
- An important incident was the massacre of the Armenians in 1915, occurring as the Turks forced Armenians from their homeland to prevent a nationalist rising in support of Russia.
- Political ideas were exacerbated by an atmosphere of military crisis, political hatred, bureaucratic contempt, wartime scarcity, and much ethnic and religious hatred.
- Armenians speak of the "forgotten genocide".

o Picking a side

- Woodrow Wilson could see little to choose between the two sides; in 1916 he offered mediation, but both sides rejected compromise.
- Re-elected on the slogan "He kept us out of war," Wilson continued to argue neutrality and supported "peace without victory."

The Collapse of Russia and the Intervention of the US

o The Withdrawal of Russia and the Treaty of Brest-Litovsk

- The Tsarist government lost the loyalty of the people through their failure to fight the war and serve the needs of the people.
- Troops mutinied in Petrograd in the midst of strikes, and the government collapsed. Nicholas II abdicated and a Provisional Government (liberal nobles, middle class intellectuals who were democrats and constitutionalists) took over.
- This new government continued the unpopular war and talked of "democracy."
  - Ordinary Russians turned to socialism, from non-Marxist to Menshevik moderates to Bolshevik extremists.
- Germany allowed Lenin to travel from his Swiss exile to Petrograd to promote revolution. The ultimate result was the Bolshevik coup d'etat (November 1917).

o The Bolsheviks pulled out of the war

- To appease the people and from convictions about the "imperialist war." The Peace of Brest-Litovsk was signed in March, 1918, stripped most of western Russia: Baltic coast, Poland, Finland, and the Ukraine.

- For Germany, the treaty ended the two-front war and provided additional supplies from such areas as the Ukraine.
- Germany soon began a major new offensive on the Western front, and by June 1 the German army was again on the Marne.

o The United States and the War

- The US was divided but tended to support the Allies, especially after the Russian Revolution. The German military decided to make an all-out effort against Britain, over civilian leadership objections.
- Germany knew the US would enter the war, but they calculated that US help would be too late. Unrestricted submarine war in early February, and ship losses, the action of German agents in the US, and the Zimmerman Note brought the US into the war in April, 1917.
- Losses were heavy at first, but new anti-sub tactics and the use of convoys proved effective.
- Meanwhile, the continuation of attrition tactics led to a mutiny of French troops and the Battle of Caporetto in Italy brought huge losses of manpower and territory.
- The US began a draft, but training was slow. Major war loans boosted the US economy as ships were built, supplies sent. Civilian rationing including day-light savings, prohibition, Victory Gardens and Meatless Tuesdays.

o The Allies created a unified command under Marshall Foch.

- US troops arrived in division strength by June, 1918, with US Marines in action at Chateau-Thierry.
- German civilians were beginning to seek peace, but the high command called for one last gamble.
- The attack was halted in the Second Battle of the Marne, and the Allies quickly launched a counterattack, spearheaded by 9 fresh US divisions.
- The arrival of fresh US divisions led Germany to negotiate, and the Armistice was signed on November 11, 1918.
- Four years of heavy losses, severe civilian suffering, and the arrival of US troops turned the tide.

- The Collapse of the Austrian and German Empires

o Austria collapsed immediately; the last emperor abdicated (11/12/17) and the Austrian empire disintegrated into its component states.

o Ludendorff was ready to quit on September 30 and called for a new, democratic government; Liberal Prince Max of Baden formed a cabinet.

- The army thus unloaded the guilt for defeat onto the new government.

- Wilson helped, insisting on dealing with the "true representatives" of the German people.

- The German navy mutinied at Kiel, and worker/soldier councils were forming; a general strike was called, and the Kaiser abdicated and fled to Holland. Germany was a republic, and the war was over.

- The people wanted only peace and the avoidance of revolution.

- The German army was still at the front; thus was born the lie that the army had been "stabbed in the back" by a socialist/Jewish government.

The Economic and Social Impact of the War

- Effects on Capitalism: Government-Regulated Economies
  - Older capitalism was laissez faire,
    - By 1914 tariffs, national industries, imperialism, and social legislation produced radical changes:
    - The "planned economy" was prevalent by 1916; economies were run by boards and commissions designed to coordinate the war effort.
  - Competition was seen as wasteful, private enterprise too slow, profits non-patriotic.
  - Control of finances, raw materiel, labor, prices.
  - Everyone was part of the war effort; women were hired by factories, with new jobs open for the first time.

- Foreign trade
  - Was controlled, with US trade tripling as European exports almost ceased.
  - Europe also needed huge loans and much US stock was sold off by Europeans.
  - The US for the first time became a creditor nation.
  - Germany had to become self-sufficient, with tight controls administered by Walter Rathenau, the industrialist who organized the German war effort.
  - In Britain, efficiency resulted in incredible outputs of war goods.

- Inflation, Industrial Changes, Control of Ideas
  - With heavy demand, taxes were not enough; governments printed money, forced credit, sold bonds--and the result was price inflation.
    - Hardest hit were middle class savers.
  - Heavy debts ultimately meant reversal of export-import balance, and a lower living standard.

- With Europe out of action, the rest of the world increased industrialization especially the US and Japan, but also Brazil, Argentina, and India.
  - Propaganda and censorship
    - Used on a huge scale.
      - Both sides blamed the other, and facts were scarce; raising doubts was unpatriotic. Civilians were stressed: war casualties, hard work, poor food, and a major effort to keep emotions at a high pitch (shades of Orwell's *1984*).
      - The enemy was portrayed as a fiend, evil incarnate--and out to control the world.
      - These ideas became major obstacles in the peace making process

The Peace of Paris

- **Fourteen Points and Treaty of Versailles**
- Winter 1918: five treaties are signed (Versailles is most significant)
- Everyone agrees that US ended war, and looked to Wilson as the messiah
- **Wilson's Fourteen Points**: January 1918
  - End to secret treaties and diplomacy
  - Freedom of the seas
  - Removal of trade barriers
  - Reduction in armaments
  - Adjustment of colonial problems
  - Evacuation of occupied territory
  - **Self-determination** of nationalities
  - Redrawing boundaries along national lines
  - International political organization to end wars
  - This is the essence of democracy, liberalism, nationalism.
- But the French wanted reparations and British needed naval power.
- Decisions made by **Big Four: Wilson, Clemenceau, Orlando, George**
- Wilson insists on **League of Nations** (to prevent war), but it ends up being a compromise
- **Provisions of Treaty of Versailles**
- Anglo-French-American guarantee treaty (if they are threatened by Germany), but this does not work out
- Alsace and Lorraine returned to France, Saar coal would go to France; Rhineland would be demilitarized and occupied
- In order to set up a buffer state against Bolshevik Russia: Poland is created
- Italy got nothing

- China walked out of the conference!

- Austrians and Sudeten German want to be annexed with Germany, but ***Anschluss*** (union of Austria and Germany) is prohibited. Sudeten Bohemia became part of Czechoslovakia.

- Germany is stripped of its colonies, which are given as **mandates** to Allies through League, but Allies dispute over who gets what (imperialists)

- Limited German army (but not for long!)

- Huge and limitless **reparations** demanded of Germany. Because of this, Germany will no longer be an exporter and it's economy will suffer.

- To justify reparations: Germany's **war guilt clause**, which increased German agitation

- Germans refused to sign until they were threatened

- Other treaties also passed!
  - Seven new independent states: Finland, Estonia, Latvia, Lithuania, Poland, Czechoslovakia, Yugoslavia (for most part, South Slavs are satisfied)
  - Romania and Greece are enlarged
  - Ottoman Empire disappears: Turkish Republic, Syria and Lebanon (French mandates), Palestine and Iraq (British mandates)

- <u>**Significance of the Treaty of Versailles**</u>
  - **Self-determination** in the new Europe: every people set up their own sovereign and independent national states
    - Populations were mixed, so there existed many problems with minorities (leads to Munich crisis)
      - Treaty too severe to conciliate the Germans and too lenient to destroy their power – loss of faith in their own treaty
      - Because of division of Allies and increasing fear of Bolshevism, Germany will later easily be able to violate the treaty
      - US rejects Treaty, and increases isolationism: this hurts prospects for peace, angered French
      - Treaty was a blow to monarchy, victory for democracy, but it did not offer solutions to basic issues (industrialism, nationalism), no guarantees for economic security or international stability
  - **League of Nations** in Geneva
    - US never joined
    - Ineffectual
    - People saw it as a way to maintain the British/French status quo
      - What's coming up?

- ○ Weak European nations face the increasing economic power of US
- ○ USSR is established
- ○ Anti-colonial movements in Asia and Africa

CHAPTER 8
END OF IMPERIAL RUSSIA & BIRTH OF THE USSR

Origins

- Alexander III takes over Russia after his father was assassinated
- He tries to stamp out revolution, silence all opposition to the government;
- Revolutionaries are driven into exile
- Jews experience pogroms
- **Pobedonostsev**
- Attacks western rationalism and liberalism, dreamed of a holy Russia as a churchly community, disciplined clergy
    - In practical terms, Russia actually was westernizing
- Russian novel
    - Tolstoy (writes *Anna Karenina* and *The Death of Ivan Ilyich*), Turgenev, Dostoevski
- Russian music spread to Europe
    - Tchaikovsky and Rimsky-Korsakov
- Russia experienced an industrial revolution, becoming an integral part of the world economy
- Thus, western ideas of democracy and freedom spread into Russia
- With industrialization came harsh working conditions and long hours in the factory
    - Unions and strikes were prohibited
    - It was easy for workers to organize and mobilize since Russian industry was heavily concentrated (all in one place)
    - Most industry was owned by foreign capital (western countries had around FOUR BILLION dollars invested in Russia prior to 1914)
- Rising business class forms Constitutional Democrat party (i.e., "Cadets"); liberals, progressives and constitutionalists, all want a nationally elected parliament to control state policies
- Peasantry lived a difficult existence
    - Still paid high taxes

- - Couldn't leave the *mirs* without permission
  - Land was divided and re-divided among peasant households
- The west was dependent on Russian cereals; often the peasants would produce a lot of food but it would end up getting exported, so they would go hungry
  - Causes "land hunger"
  - Kulaks - landowners/wealthier peasants
- Pugachev (1773) and Razin were famous peasant rebels; inspire the peasants to demand and obtain credit from the government to buy land in order to appease their land hunger.
- Intelligentsia caused a lot of disturbances; formed secret societies engaged in outwitting the police, spent time discussing and reforming doctrines.
- **Agents**
- Pobiedonostsev
- Alexander III
- Count Witte-1897, Russia adopts the gold standard to make currency convertible
- Pugachev and Razin
- Plekhanov and Axelrod found Russian Social Democrat/Marxist party
- Lenin - Foresaw the possibility of a proletarian dictatorship to represent the conscious wishes of a small vanguard and might be able to impose itself upon the masses.
- Most of revolutionary intelligentsia were **populists**
  - Generally had mystical faith in undeveloped strength of Russian people
  - Interested in peasant problems
  - Believed in Pugachev's Rebellion in 1773; inspired them to proclaim a revolution!
  - Favored strengthening the *mir* and equalizing the peasant's share of it
  - A populist was the first to translate *The Communist Manifesto* into Russian (shows their devotion to Marx & Engels)
  - Felt revolution would come soon since capitalism would implode
  - **1901 -** they form the **Social Revolutionary party**
- **Plekhanov and Axelrod** founded the **Russian Social Democratic (Marxist) party** in **1883** while in exile
  - young Lenin & his wife Krupskaya were Marxists
  - much of the revolutionary intelligentsia turned from populism to Marxism since factory workers were revolting more than peasants
  - included **Lenin, Trotsky and Stalin (major Marxists)**
- **Lenin, while** in Siberia, lived a happy life with other exiles (they played chess, debated, had sleepovers...the opposite of what will be experienced once the communists come to power).

- o His intellectual vigor, irresistible drive, and shrewdness as a tactician led him to become a major force in the Marxist party
- **1898,** Marxists in Russia founded the **Social Democratic Labor Party**
  - o More inclined to see the revolution as an international movement
  - o They expected the world revolution to break out first in western Europe
  - o Admired German Social Democratic party
  - o Tended to think that Russia must develop **capitalism, an industrialist proletariat, and a modern form of class struggle** in order to precipitate a revolution
  - o Looked upon the peasantry with suspicion, ridiculed the mir, and hated the social revolutionaries
- So let's recap: **Social Revolutionaries** favor <u>peasants</u>; **Social Democrats** favor the <u>industrial working class</u>
- Russian Marxists hold party congress in Brussels and London in **1903**
  - o The **purpose** was to unify all Russian Marxism (but it ended up splitting it forever)
  - o **Bolshevik** (majority) <u>versus</u> **Menshevik** (minority)
  - o Lenin becomes the founder of Bolshevism, organized itself as a party in **1912**
- **Bolsheviks**
  - o "Hard-liners" attracted to Lenin
  - o Party should be a small revolutionary elite, with a hard core of reliable and zealous workers
  - o Believed in centralized party; central committee would determine the doctrine and control all personnel involved in the party
  - o ***Stood for the reaffirmation of the fundamentals of Marxism (dialectical materialism and irreconcilable class struggle)***
- **Mensheviks (the "more compliant with the enemy capitalist" minority)**
  - o Wished for a larger and more open party with membership for sympathizers
  - o Favored degree of influence from the members, not a committee
  - o Came to recommend cooperation with liberals, progressives, and bourgeois democrats
  - o Came to resemble Marxists of western Europe
- Lenin's beliefs
  - o Capitalism exploited the workers
  - o History was shaped by economic forces and was moving towards socialism
  - o Class struggle was the law of society

- o Existing forms of religion, government, philosophy and morals were weapons of the ruling class
  - o Lenin denounced all who tired to add anything to Marxism
  - o Imperialism: it was exclusively a product of monopoly capitalism which is bent on exporting surplus capital and investing it in undeveloped areas for greater profits
- The party was an organization in which intellectuals provided leadership and understanding for workers, who could not help themselves
  - o Task of intellectuals was to make the trade union and the workers more class-conscious and revolutionary
  - o Intellectuals represented the "brains"; workers represented the "brawn"
- There were many attempts at reform and westernization preceding the revolution of 1917
  - o Can be seen in the Revolution of 1905
- All three of the new parties were propaganda agencies
  - o Had to do all their work underground
  - o After 1900, growing signs of popular unrest
- **Nicholas II** - Tsar, very narrow outlook, denounced questioning the autocracy, Orthodoxy, and Great Russian nationalism as un-Russian; abhorred democracy
- Chief minister **Plehve**: hoped short and successful war with Japan would create more attachment to the government (obviously failed)
  - o Liberals began to believe that the government's immunity to criticism and secret methods made them inefficient, unable to win a war or modernize Russia economically (but there was little they could do).
- **Father Gapon** - allowed to go among St. Petersburg workers to organize them and counter revolutionary propaganda
- However, the peasants believed that appealing directly to the Tsar would help
  - o They drew up a petition for 8-hr work day, minimum wage of 1 ruble, dissolving of bureaucracy, and a representative form of government
  - o Unarmed and peacefully they marched to Tsar's Winter Palace in 1905; troops opened fire on the demonstrators (**"Bloody Sunday"**)
- A wave of political strikes erupted due to this violent response by the autocracy!
  - o **"Soviets"** or councils of workers were formed
  - o Peasants began overrunning the lands of the gentry
  - o Everyone agreed that a more democratic and representative government was necessary for Russia
- St. Petersburg Soviets declared a general strike in October 1905, spreading to other cities

- o Tsar issues his **October Manifesto promising:** constitution, civil liberties, and a Duma elected by all classes (it would have the power to enact laws and control the administration). Promises won't be kept.
  - ▪ The point of the manifesto was to divide the opposition. Constitutional Democrats (Cadets) hoped that social problems could be dealt with through negotiation, while aroused peasants and workers were not yet satisfied (wanted more land, less taxes, shorter working day, better wages)
- o They all believed (correctly) that the October Manifesto was an act of deception!
- Created the Duma, but the Tsar announced in 1906 that it would have no power over foreign policy, the budget, or government personnel
  - o Tsar Nicholas II (until his abdication in 1917) would NEVER allow public participation in the government
- Organization of the **Black Hundreds (ultra-nationalists):** upheld autocracy and the Orthodox church, terrorized revolutionary peasants, killed jews, and urged the monarchy to boycott the Duma
- Socialists refused to recognize it and urged workers to boycott it in favor of a more representative government
- The Duma (there were 4)
  - o #1- Formed in 1906; elected by unequal voting, Cadets demand true universal male suffrage, Tsar responds by dismissing the Duma
  - o #2- Formed in 1907; government controlled elections by suppressing party meetings and newspapers, Cadets become willing to cooperate with gov't, but it ended when the gov't arrested about 50 socialists for being "revolutionaries bent on destruction"
  - o #3- 1907 to 1912
  - o #4- 1912 to 1916
- **Peter Stolypin-** reformer whose goal was to build up the propertied classes as friends of the state (he was behind the dissolving of the first two Dumas)
  - o favored & broadened the powers of provincial *zemstvos*
  - o allowed peasants to sell their shares of communal land and to leave their villages
  - o HIS POLICY WAS SUCCESSFUL!
    - ▪ Between 1907 and 1916, 6.2 million families were allowed to apply for separation from the *mir*
    - ▪ Trend toward individual property and independent farming
  - o However, land shortage was still prevalent, kulaks were resented
  - o Tsar did not give him enough support and reactionaries detested his Western orientation, Marxists feared his reforms would do away with agrarian discontent that made up their support system

- o Stolypin was assassinated by a secret agent of the reactionary Tsarist police!
- Despite all the oppression of the Russian public, Westernization was on the horizon
    - o Industries were growing and railroads were expanding
    - o Private property and capitalism spread to more people
    - o A kind of parliamentary system was adopted (Duma)
    - o Bolshevik party paper, *Pravda* begun in St. Petersburg in 1912
- So, to **what extent, and with what results were there attempts at reform and westernization in a context of increasing violence and repression up to the revolution of 1917?**
    - o Politically: there were attempts at reform to a great extent; results were not very helpful (Duma and its constant dissolution)
    - o Socially: to a great extent there were attempts at reform, results actually made a difference in the lives of many people (Stolypin's reforms)
- WWI required the full and willing cooperation of government and people because of its "total" nature
    - o However, national minorities were unaffected, socialists were uncooperative (unlike their "brothers" in Germany and France), and ordinary working men and peasants marched off to war with little sense of purpose.
    - o The middle class cooperated but was angered by glaring government mismanagement and the military disasters of 1914 and 1915.
    - o Provincial *zemstvos* organized to mobilize agriculture and industry; business groups formed to maximize production -- giving the middle class a sense of strength and making them more critical of the bureaucracy.
    - o Tsarina Alexandra was perceived as conceited and hated; she thought she was superior to Russians outside her circle, and had a great amount of influence over Nicholas.
        - Rasputin gained influence over her because of his "powers" over young Nicholas, and his control of access to the royal family separated the Tsar from both the people and his own government.
    - o By March of 1917 Russia was in crisis, especially in Petrograd.
        - The Third Duma and Fourth Dumas were suspended for their critical attitude towards Rasputin and towards the conduct of the war.
        - Food was scarce, and there were no price controls or rationing; food riots on March 8 escalated into insurrection which the army refused to suppress.
        - A Soviet of Workers' and Soldiers' Deputies was formed; it became the center of working-class upheaval.

- - The Duma was disbanded, but it set up an executive committee; on March 14 it began a Provisional Government under Prince Lvov and supported by Alexander Kerensky, a moderate Social Revolutionary.
    - Nicholas tried to return to Petrograd from the front, but the army stopped his train. He now abdicated; when the Grand Duke refused the throne, Russia became a Republic.
- **The Bolshevik Revolution: November, 1917:**
    - The Provisional Government called for an election for a Constituent Assembly. Pushed by the desperate Allies, it also attempted a war offensive in July.
    - The armies at the front deserted in mass; peasants overran rural districts; the Petrograd Soviet called for an end to the war and issued Order No. 1 calling for the command of the army by elected committees.
    - Lenin arrived in Petrograd in April and threw Bolshevik support to the Soviets.
    - A n attempted military coup **failed**; the Bolsheviks were **blamed**; Kerensky was now named head of the Provisional government; General Kornilov, newly appointed military commander, attempted his own coup but was defeated by socialists led by the Bolsheviks.
      - Kerensky and the Provisional Government were blamed for problems and lost prestige.
      - Worsening food shortages in Petrograd, with the failure of transport plus farm turmoil, brought daily crises.
- Lenin concentrated on four points:
    - **Peace**, the end to the war;
    - **Land** to the peasants who tilled it;
    - **Socialist ownership of the means of production**;
    - **Recognition of the Soviets as the government** all under the superb tactical slogan "Peace, Land, Bread." The Bolsheviks had a majority in the Soviets; the time was ripe for a coup.
- With the support of key army and navy units, the Bolsheviks on the night of November 6 captured telephone exchanges, railroad stations, and electric lighting plants; a warship turned its guns on the Winter Palace.
    - The Congress of Soviets ousted the Duma and replaced it with a Council of People's Commissars, headed by **Lenin** and with **Trotsky** as commissar for foreign affairs, **Stalin** commissar for nationalities.
    - Lenin announced two resolutions, calling for an end to the war, "without annexations, without indemnities" and abolishing landlord property.
    - When the Constituent Assembly finally met, it was adjourned by armed Bolsheviks; the "dictatorship of the proletariat" had begun.
- The Civil War

- Lenin now made the Treaty of Brest-Litovsk with Germany, assuming that the proletarian revolution would break out soon in Europe.
    - Russia lost its Baltic States, plus Ukraine and Poland of (which Germany already occupied).
    - The peace gave Lenin leadership over Russia, but threw the country into civil war.
- Resistance formed under a variety of banners - bourgeois liberals, *zemstov* men, Constitutional Democrats, Mensheviks and Social Revolutionaries.
    - All obtained aid from the Allies in hopes of renewing the Eastern Front. The Bolsheviks created the Cheka, a political police which was the predecessor of the NKVD and later the KGB.
    - Trotsky, as War Commissar, created the Red Army. Lenin played a tactical game, declaring "War Communism," a mix of expedience and arid principle which nationalized heavy industry and put smaller corporations under worker committees.
        - Food was requisitioned by city workers sent into the countryside.
- The gentry organized armies on the Don River, under Deniken and Kornilov; the Social Republicans organized in the Volga, backed by a Czech legion of 45,000. U.S. and British forces took Murrnansk and Archangel, with the Japanese in Vladivostok (Eastern Russia).
- One hope was that a force could cross Siberia, join with the Czechs, break up Bolshevism, and reopen the Eastern Front.
- The Bolsheviks first fought the Germans in the Ukraine -- and then the French, who occupied Odessa after Germany's defeat. They re-conquered the Ukraine, Armenia, Georgia, and Azerbaijan; defeated the "White Army" under Rangel in the South, and defeated Kolchak in Siberia.
- In 1920 they fought the Poles, who had invaded the Ukraine arid Byelorussia.
- Bolsheviks won because all the various anti-Bolshevik forces were not successful in their rally against them.
- Trotsky forged a disciplined Red Army under political commissars; the Bolsheviks could also appeal to peasant invaders and win support by distributing land.
- The end of the beginning...
    - By **1922**, the Bolsheviks controlled the vast majority of the old Tsarist territory, except for the Baltic States, Bessarabia (Romania), and parts of Byelorussia (Poland).
    - Peace had been won; the regime still stood. The cost had been heavy loss of life in the Red Terror, partly a response to civil and foreign war and

partly a campaign to exterminate "bourgeois" opponents and even "leftist deviationists."

- o The human toll was appalling, but the slate was cleared for Lenin's new communist society.

- Terror was most definitely used as a mean of consolidating power and eliminating dissent.

  - o Thousands of Russians were shot merely as hostages, and other thousands were killed without even the summary formalities of revolutionary tribunals.

  - o The Cheka was the most formidable political police that had yet appeared. The Bolshevik Terror was aimed at the physical extermination of all who opposed the new regime.

  - o A bourgeois class background would go far to confirm the guild of the person charged with conspiring against the Soviet state.

  - o As the head of the Cheka said: "The first questions you should put to the accused persons are, to what class does he belong, what is his origin, what was his education, and what is his profession?"

    - ▪ These should determine the fate of the accused.

    - ▪ This is the essence of the Red Terror.

  - o The Terror struck at the revolutionaries themselves quite as much as it did the Bourgeoisie; it was to continue to do so long after the revolution was secure.

  - o The Terror succeeded in its purpose.

    - ▪ Together with the victories of the Red Army, it established the new regime.

    - ▪ No "bourgeois" presumed to be permitted to take part in Russian politics.

- The Purge Trials of the 1930s were led by Joseph Stalin.

  - o Assassination of Sergey Kirov removed an enemy and provided Stalin with the excuse to launch the purge trials of the late 1930s.

    - ▪ The Bolshevik party was purged ruthlessly with expulsion of one-third its members.

    - ▪ Numerous old Bolshevik leaders were tried, forced to confess, and executed along with Lenin's friend Bukharin.

    - ▪ Leaders of the highest party and military rank and unknown millions of lesser figures were purged, to be executed or to disappear deep within the Gulag.

  - o The USSR was now run by "new men," products of the new order, loyal to Stalin.

    - ▪ At least 786,098 (but clearly MANY more) were recorded as being executed in the "Great Terror".

- o Stalin killed anyone that had any association with Vladimir Lenin. By these purges Stalin's dictatorship was reinforced.
- Lenin and Trotsky made many important additions to Marxist thought.
  - o Lenin by supporting (will become known as Marxism-Leninism) a view where dialectical materialism was accepted as a philosophy – and to some extent, a religion.
    - Citizens learned to take orders without question and submit to authoritative leadership immediately (i.e., "party discipline").
    - The function of the party, as defined in a Marxist sense, was to carry out the dictatorship of the proletariat.
    - It can be said that Lenin managed to fully organize the communists in Russia and was able to largely establish Marxist thought among the people.
- Lenin dies of a stroke, Trotsky tried to take over.
  - o Trotsky created a policy of "permanent revolution", a never-ending drive for proletarian objectives on all fronts in all parts of the world (an idea that Mao Zedong will adopt).
    - He championed world revolution and denounced bureaucracy.
    - He called for more forceful development in industry and the collectivization of agriculture.
    - Trotsky asked for the immediate adoption of this plan, but was unable to win the party's support, like the articulate Lenin before him.
- Federal republic of different nationalities
  - o Federal principle was to answer the problem of nationalism and led to increased cultural nationalism
    - Different cultural groups are autonomous, but still are united together in the union (in reality only in paper in the USSR)
    - Constitution of 1936: created Soviet of Nationalities: representatives (on varying levels of importance) from each area
  - o However, the USSR is still very Slavic: most of its population lives in the three Slavic soviet republics
- Political and economic rights were still limited by the Party
  - The Communist Party has the real power
  - Minority grievances are unresolved
- Supposed parallelism between the two, but really the party controls the state so much that it becomes meaningless
  - o State
    - Basic unit is council (soviet)
    - Ascending hierarchy: town=provincial; public=national

- - - Seemingly more democratic: Constitution of 1936: all citizens have right to vote, direct vote for delegates, secret ballot, bicameral parliament
  - ○ Communist Party
    - - Authority begins at the top, proceeds downward (principle of democratic centrism, once a decision has been reached, party discipline is expected)
    - - Headed by Central Committee, which functions through:
    - - Secretary: fashioned by Stalin – organizational matters
    - - Politburo: political bureau of chief legislators that discusses policy and personnel
  - ○ In theory, members are elected democratically, but really they have to be approved by the party
  - ○ The Politburo is a small group of Communist Party members that control everyone and everything!
  - ○ **It must be a disciplined group to preserve party unity once the party grows (purge the disloyal or ideologically suspect)**
- Old Bolsheviks (from before 1917) vs. Careerists (new people wanting to join Soviets)
  - ○ Old Bolsheviks require strict conformity to the Party so they maintain control and careerists do not take over
- Everyone has to study Marxism and Leninism
- The Party restricts originality, boldness, freedom of thought
- Lenin's New Economic Policy (NEP): somewhat successful infusion of capitalism to keep the USSR afloat economically
- Background:
  - ○ Peasants were angry because: war communism, severe drought and breakdown of transportation which led to famine, killing 4-5 million people
  - ○ Increasing chaos and disillusionment with communism
  - ○ Result was NEP – Lenin realizes he needs to pacify the people
- NEP: instead of the government owning all businesses, people are now encouraged to conduct private trading for profit
- Effects!
  - ○ New commercial class (neo-bourgeoisie) develops – no classless society as promised earlier!
  - ○ Peasants become "proletarians": wage-earning hired hands
  - ○ Middlemen can buy/sell farm and city products at market prices
  - ○ This system favored big farmers (kulaks)

- o LONG TERM: brings Russia roughly up to economic levels of 1914, but there is no real progress yet because they have just recovered from crises caused by revolution in 1917
- o These ideas actually go against communist principles, so even if the NEP may have helped the USSR economically, it did not help the vision of a proletarian dictatorship
- Stalin's Five Year Plans - more in sync with communist thought
  - o Rapid industrialization and collectivization of agriculture through a centrally planned economy (these were originally Trotsky's ideas)
  - o Deviates from doctrine to model USSR after planned European economies of WWI
  - o Gosplan: planning agency – determined how much of everything should be produced
  - o Sought to control what was regulated by supply and demand in capitalist societies
  - o Many errors, unmanageable, bureaucratic paperwork, and inefficiency!
- In order to build up industry without foreign loans (i.e., the British model), they needed a substantial increase in agricultural production!
  - o Collective farms are created (shift back to focus of communism, instead of NEP)
  - o Kulaks are destroyed as a class because of this – Kulaks kill their own livestock to prevent the soviets from seizing it for the state – brings on yet another famine
  - o Decreased production, but there are still high quotas because the government must have a trade surplus. Peasants go without food if they cannot fulfill the quota.
  - o A return to the *mir* way of life
  - o The policy increases industrialization, even though it heightens tensions between classes, and results in repression and famine
- Society – not successful/flawed vision
  - o Women's rights
    - A classless society should in theory get rid of gender hierarchies
    - Women receive equal voting rights, divorce rights, and access to birth control and abortions
    - These were only rights theoretically – the government went back on its word (but education did increase for women)
  - o The arts
    - Rejection of traditional ideas and artistic forms – social upheaval
    - Radical artists combined "futurist" art with social revolution

- The period of experimentation in 1920s was brief: only "social realism" celebrating the revolution, factory production, and Marxist policies is permitted

- Social Costs overall
  - Heavy sacrifices demanded from the people
  - Liquidation of kulaks and all who oppose the system
  - Use of forced labor – long hours, low wages
  - Self-denial (of food, resources): sacrifice for the revolution to succeed
  - Use of propaganda to control people
  - Overall standard of living increases will increase somewhat by the 1930s, but WWII is just around the corner!
  - The "problems" of capitalism disappear:
    - No unemployment
    - No cycles of boom and depression
    - Theoretically, no upper classes existed, although government officials, managers, engineers, some artists/intellectuals got the most rewards (will develop into apparatchik and nomenklatura
  - Incentives for increased production
    - 1935 – miner Stakhanov increased output of coal and thus earned bonuses. Other workers copied him and they were all known as "labor heroes" – higher stage of socialist competition
    - Helped production (some tried to copy him, but suspected government propaganda ploy)! Incentives are much less than in capitalist societies.
    - Managers are also under competitive pressure – if they failed, they were obviously betraying socialism
  - The Meaning of "Socialist Solidarity":
    - No skepticism or opposition was tolerated (purges!)
    - No unions or free press
    - No political parties (only the CPSU)
    - Art, literature, and science are used for political propaganda
    - Dialectical materialism is the official philosophy
    - Conformity everywhere
- The Third International – Background (1919)
  - Zinoviev is President
  - Met in Moscow, so it was dominated by Lenin and his Soviets
  - Became known as the Communist International (aka Comintern)

- It became very centralized – international members were strict communists taking orders from Moscow – strong
- Influence on other (colonized) regions
- Key provisions of Lenin's Twenty-one Points:
    - Each national party must call itself Communist
    - No more "reformist" socialism
    - Propaganda for labor unions
    - Infiltrate the armies
    - Discipline the members (must submit to international orders)
    - No respect for parliamentary democracy
    - A call for revolution – believed class revolution was near!
    - Promoted world revolution
- Zimmerwald program: called for the end of WWI without reparations or indemnities because they wanted to get on with the revolution! Many Marxist ideologues believed the war would eventually lead to world-wide class revolution
    - Became a source of inspiration for communists throughout the world – colonized regions looked to USSR as an example of how a society could modernize without resorting to capitalism or foreign guidance
- Increasing influence in Asia (which was still under European spheres of influence)
- USSR is able to control Eastern Europe through these ideas
- This was the start of fascism
- 1927: Stalin begins to focus on building up socialism in one country
- Comintern instructs all communists to form coalitions with socialists/liberals in "popular fronts" in order to support communists within their own country
- 1943: Comintern is abolished (appease Britain and U.S.)
- Marxism is now an actual movement, not just a branch of thought

CHAPTER 9

THE POST WWI WORLD

Political difficulties following WWI

- President Wilson had stated that the reason for the war was to make the world safe for democracy
  - This led to advances in political democracy throughout the world.
  - New states emerged, adopting written constitutions and universal suffrage.
    - Great Britain passed universal MALE suffrage in 1918.
    - FEMALE suffrage in 1918 Great Britain; total political equality by 1928.
    - 1920 in the U.S. Women were also able to vote in Germany and the rest of Eastern Europe
    - Women in the Soviet Union had full suffrage by 1917.
  - The socialist parties of Eastern Europe gained political momentum; they called themselves Communists. Labor unions grew in membership, prestige, and importance; all fueled by the confidence that resulted from their involvement in the war.
  - Social legislation came with the rise in socialism; an eight-hour working day became the norm, government-sponsored insurance was enacted against sickness, accident, and old age.
  - The only exception to these gains was Italy, where democracy experienced a sharp setback due to the rise of fascism.
  - In 1922 Benito Mussolini would take over and create a Fascist, single-state and autocratic Italy.
- The new postwar states underwent some modification and their governments underwent considerable reorganization after the war.
  - The new states were **accidents of the war**, nowhere did they represent revolutionary sentiment.
  - New nations had a small middle class and a peasant mass only recently freed—and most were economically backward.

- They set up protective tariffs and attempted to develop factories—but the tariffs cut the circulation of goods and protected **inefficient** industries.
  - Older, established industry, especially in Vienna and Prague, were hurt. Agrarian reform was attempted, in order to create a small peasant class on the French model.
  - In the Baltic States, the old German aristocrats lost their land; in Czechoslovakia, German landlords also lost land.
  - A less thorough effort was made in Rumania and Yugoslavia. Finland, Bulgaria, and Greece did not need reform.
  - Poland and Hungary had exceptionally strong landed magnates who were able to deflect change.
- The republicans, moderate socialists, agrarians, or nationalists who now found themselves in power had to **improvise** governments for which there had been little preparation.
  - They had to contend with reactionaries, monarchists, and members of the old aristocracy.
    - The new states embodied the principle of national self-determination, holding that every nationality should enjoy political sovereignty.
  - They set out to make themselves democratic. However, the whole Eastern bloc was lagging behind western Europe due to their involvement in agriculture and non-modern industry, factories, railroads, cities, literacy, schooling, health, life expectancy and standard of living.
- The new states then set out to modernize themselves by introducing democratic and constitutional ideas, protective tariffs, finding new frontiers of trade, and reform of land ownership.
  - The whole agrarian base of society became overturned and small farms became the predominant form of land ownership.
  - Despite all these land reforms, they failed to solve basic economic problems; peasants lacked capital, agricultural skill, and knowledge of the market.
  - Therefore, farm productivity **did not rise**. The new states remained frustrated by their inability to mingle with democracy.
- The supreme question for Germany after the war was how Germany would adjust to the post-war conditions.
  - The Weimar Republic and Treaty of Versailles were products of the defeat of Germany.
  - No one in Germany accepted the treaty or the new conditions as final.
  - The Germans had only signed under **pressure** from the Allies; they saw it as **diktat**, or a dictated peace, especially due to the 'war guilt' clause it contained which offended the German sense of honor.

- o Neither the reparations demanded of them, nor the new frontiers, were accepted by the Germans as settled.
- The French lived in fear of the day when Germany would recover politically and especially militarily, so they began to form alliances against Germany with Poland, Czechoslovakia, and other East European states and insisted on German payment of reparations.
  - o The French, blocked in the attempt to collect reparations and assisted by the Belgians, sent units of French army to occupy Ruhr Valley in 1923.
  - o The German sense of honor was outraged; neither reparations nor the eastern frontier was regarded as settled.
  - o France had desired guarantees—either the cession of the Rhineland or the guarantee of the frontier by the US and Britain—but the US senate had rejected both Versailles and the treaty of guarantee, only desiring a strong Germany as a good customer.
    - The League, with every nation having a veto, offered little hope—so the French turned to reparations. In 1921 the Reparations Commission set the sum at the astronomical sum of **$35 billion**.
  - o Germany, in response, looked to the USSR—and the result was the Treaty of Rapallo of 1922. The USSR was to receive manufactured goods from Germany, while German officers and technicians instructed the Red Army. Thus the German army was able to maintain a high standard of training and technical knowledge.
- The Germans respond with strikes. At the same time, the Weimar republic kept printing paper money; Germany had suffered **mass inflation** during and after the war.
  - o Blocked from collecting reparations, France sent army units to occupy the Ruhr. Germans resisted by general strikes and passive resistance—with workers benefits provided by merely printing money.
    - The result was catastrophic inflation, wiping out all paper value, annuities, pensions, insurance policies, savings accounts, income from bonds and mortgages.
    - The middle class was pauperized
    - Paper money was worthless; 4 trillion paper marks was equal to 1 US dollar.
    - A social revolution was under way as debtors paid off creditors using worthless money; all forms of revenue were devalued.
    - The middle class lost faith in society and in Germany itself.
- A kind of moral void was created, with nothing for them to believe in, hope for, or respect.
  - o Still, the German economy was able to reset itself. In 1924 the US initiated the **Dawes plan** to assure the flow of reparations.
  - o The French would evacuate the Ruhr, reparations payments were cut down, and Germany was allowed to borrow abroad.

- ○ American capital was invested in Germany; Germany was slowly getting put back on its feet.
- ○ The Weimar republic enjoyed a brief period of prosperity up until the Great Depression of 1929.
- **Golden Years** in the Weimar Republic were 1924-1929
  - ○ None of the issues from Versailles were directly dealt with (if they were dealt with, they might have avoided bigger problems later on!)
  - ○ Constant threat of Germany: there was still a fear that Germany would overthrow the other nations by force.
- To reduce pressures, **Streseman** (Germany), **Briand** (France), and **MacDonald** (Britain) signed the **Locarno Pacts in 1925**.
  - ○ These marked the highest point of international calm between the two world wars.
  - ○ Germany would guarantee the French and Belgian borders and agreed to arbitration in the East.
  - ○ France balanced German power in the East with its own diplomatic alliances: it promised to aid Czechoslovakia and Poland in case of German aggression (this would draw it into WWII) and the **Little Entente** (Czechoslovakia, Yugoslavia, and Romania) – alliance with Poland would draw it into WWII!
  - ○ Britain promised to aid France and Belgium if their borders were threatened, but made no promises to the East (isolationism).
- Effects!
  - ○ Brought great relief even if they did not lead to anything.
  - ○ In 1926, Germany joined the League of Nations
  - ○ In 1928 the **Kellogg-Briand Pact** was passed, which condemned war.
  - ○ There was a short-lived feeling of hope in the 1920s (stopped in 1930s after the Great Depression)
- **The Young Turks and the Turkish Republic**
- Creation of Turkish Republic
  - ○ With the Revolution of 1908, the Young Turks wanted to prevent the dissolution of the Ottoman Empire, but this was not to be.
  - ○ Greece wanted to advance into Turkey (the **Aegean**), and in 1915, the Allies agreed to partition Turkey
  - ○ **Mustapha Kemal** was able to drive them out with nationalist support and help from the USSR.
  - ○ Now, Constantinople became **Istanbul**
  - ○ **Turkish Republic** was proclaimed in 1923 after a nationalist revolution of the Young Turks (led by Kemal) overthrows the sultanate and caliphate (because they are associated with subservience to foreigners, inefficiency and corruption).

- Now, the Young Turks are in control, and they do essentially the same thing that Russia and other places went did – model society after Western Europe
  - Democracy is advocated (universal male suffrage, parliament, ministries, president), and the "people" (meaning the Turkish people) are sovereign
  - Other nationalities are excluded, so the Greek element was uprooted and forced back to Greece (hurts economically Greece because it now has the burden of a larger population!)
  - This homogenized Turkey and ended disputes between Turkey and Greece until after WWII.
  - The government was secularized (for the first time in a Muslim country)
  - Women receive certain rights - polygamy is outlawed
  - Western dress is advocated (no more fez!), as is the western alphabet, calendar, metric system, and surnames. Kemal becomes **Ataturk** ("great Turk")
  - The capital is moved to **Ankara**
  - Five-year development program with high tariffs is put into effect, modeled after the USSR (mines, factories, and railroads are under government ownership).
- So all in all, the Young Turks modernize the republic to become more like the west (in political and social aspects) – BUT there is still the influence of the USSR
- **India, Jewel in the Crown of the British Empire**
  - At the close of WWI, it looks as if India is on the brink of revolution, but then **Gandhi** (known as **Mahatma**, the Holy One) comes into the picture in 1919.
  - He advocates a movement for self-government, spiritual and economic independence from Britain, and NON-VIOLENCE
  - Internal tolerance between Hindus and Muslims, as well as between castes (an end to racial discrimination).
  - He stressed noncooperation, passive resistance, civil disobedience, and boycotts as methods of non-violence.
  - He refused representative institutions and industrialism, and this severely hurt British exports. The home spun movement of cotton began.
  - Ironically, the Indians want Britain to leave so they can modernize, but in some regards they move backwards economically in order to get Britain out
  - Assassinated in 1948 by a Hindu extremist who felt he was conceding to much to the Muslims.
    - The British still believed that because of the ethnic divisions in India, independence would lead to anarchy.
      - Many Indians agreed and thus stressed cooperation with Britain,

- Others, including **Nehru**, looked to Marxism and saw the USSR as a model for development.
- Again we see the influence of the USSR – some people in the developing world see socialism as a better more achievable idea, because capitalism was associated with the western imperialists
- This made the British nervous, so in the 1930s they gradually permitted increased Indian political participation and reform to try to win back their support
  - The 20 years between WWI and WWII were full of disturbances, but India did not win independence until after WWII: it was then split into a Hindu India and Muslim Pakistan, so obviously Gandhi's desire for a unified India was not to be.
- **China**
- At first the Guomindang (nationalist Party headed by Chiang Kai-shek) is supported by the Chinese Communists
  - Chiang succeeded Dr. Sun Yat Sen to the leadership of the Nationalist Party
- Chiang's main objectives were to compel the independent war lords and regime of Beijing to accept the authority of a single Nationalist government
- 1928: Chiang's army occupied Beijing and capital was moved to Nanjing
- His control was still somewhat limited by some provincial warlords
- Outside powers extended diplomatic recognition to Nanjing government and conceded its right to organize a run tariffs and customs
  - Also partially surrendered extraterritorial privileges
- 1927: open break occurred between the Guomindang and its communist left wing
  - The killing of foreigners in the North which had been executed by Communists sparked this break
  - Radical disturbances by the left frightened and alienated the wealthier and conservative members of the Guomindang
    - This jeopardized Chiang's funding for the government and army
- Chiang decided to just purge Communists and Russian advisers from the party, executing many
  - Communist uprising in Guangzhou was suppressed
  - Guerilla warfare ensued between Nationalists and Communists
    - Communists and the Chinese Red Army under the leadership of Mao Zedong
- Chiang's supporters slowly lost their sense of motivation

- o Although he had financial and military support from the Guomindang, the Nationalist leadership was often corrupt and inefficient, feared social upheaval, and saw their maintenance in power as their chief goal
  - o Chiang faced mounting dissatisfaction due to the reluctance to reform among those in his party, but he still was busy consolidating his regime
- Communists were operating in southeast China
  - o Fed on popular discontent
  - o Drew support from the peasantry by a systematic policy of redistribution of large landed estates coupled with propaganda
  - o Fought of Chiang's army
- 1931; Communists proclaim the Chinese Soviet Republic in the Southeast
  - o Nationalists succeeded in dislodging them
  - o Communists led by Mao go on the Long March
  - o Long March: 6,000 mile journey in 1934-1935
    - A retreat where Mao fought off Nationalist armies
    - Built strong following among rural masses
- Chiang was forced to end the civil war so he could defend China against Japan
  - o Nationalists and Communists form alliance of mutual convenience in 1937
  - o Red Army placed under Nationalist control (only nominally)
  - o UNITE CHINA TO EXPELL THE JAPANESE!
  - o However, there is extreme distrust and both try to conserve their forces for their eventual use when the Japanese withdraw and the civil war will resume.
- Japan's rapid modernization and expansion helped bring them into competition with the Western world
- During WWI, 21 Demands presented to China allowed Japan to obtain German concession of Shantung
- During the war industrialization of Japan continued
- Japan captured many markets while the rest of the world struggled
- After the war, remained one of the chief suppliers of textiles in Asia
  - o Could produce at lower prices than Europeans
  - o Sustained a good standard of living (import raw materials and selling manufactured goods)
- 1925- universal male suffrage
- Asians people finally were playing a major role in the world economy!
- Only in Japan of all modern countries did a constitutional law prescribe that the war and navy ministers must be active generals or admirals
- Diet (Japanese parliament) had restricted powers

- Economically, governments sponsorship of industrial growth resulted in tremendous concentration of economic powers in the hands of the Zaibatsu families
- Most restless group in Japan was the nationalist, who's revival that had cultivated Shinto emperor worship and the way of the warrior (Bushido) as a new and modern way of life.
  - Regarded imitating the West's industrialization as desirable
  - Wanted Japan to dominate all of Asia
- 1931: Japanese army units spread throughout Manchuria
  - Declared Manchuria to be an independent state under emperor Pu Yi, and renamed the state Manchukuo (it will be a puppet of Japan)
- Japan was found to have been "disturbing the peace" and was kicked out of the League of Nations
- The Revolt in Asia
  - Resentments in Asia
    - Imperialism was increasingly condemned and political consciousness was rising.
    - Asians objected to European special privilege, use of customs revenues to pay debts, exploitation of resources and labor, the threat to ancient cultures and languages, and the idea of white racial supremacy.
    - But there was also ambivalence, as they desire.
    - Western science, industry, and organization.
    - Increasingly, old monarchs were charged with subservience to the West, and replaced by national assemblies—the Persian *Majlis,* the revolt of the Young Turks in 1908, the revolution of Sun Yat Sen in 1911.
  - First World War and Russian Revolution
    - Asians were heavily involved in World War I, for example, India provided one million troops.
    - The nations were also stimulated to increasing output of raw materials.
    - With the huge investment at stake, colonial governments were forced into concessions—elected legislative assemblies, consultive bodies both elected and appointed, both European and native.
    - The Russian Revolution also provided stimulus, since colonial peoples identified capitalism with imperialism and took on a strong socialist content.
    - The Comintern under Zinoviev worked to exploit these feelings, but nationalism was the key.
- **The Great Depression: Crash of 1929 and spread of economic crisis**
  The depression began as a stock market and financial crisis

- **New York Stock Exchange** crashed in October 1929; sock values had been driven up by speculation (investors who drive up prices by buying in anticipation of rising prices, but when prices fall they have to sell off stock and repay borrowed money)
    - Stock had been bought on credit
    - "Margins" for buying stock were small
    - Weakening of stock values caused excessive selling of stock, causing stock values to drop drastically
    - Crisis spread through industry
- Export of American capital came to an end
- Americans ceased to buy foreign goods due to falling incomes
- 1931 - **Creditanstalt** (Vienna bank) failed; people could not collect money owed to them or withdraw money they had put on banks
- Unemployment reached 30 million world-wide in 1932
- When workers wages were disappeared, buying plummeted, production plummeted, and farmers income disappeared
- REACTIONS to Great Depression
- Optimists (**Hoover**) said depression would be temporary
- Others saw it as the failure of capitalism
- The most common consequence of the depression was strong movement toward **economic nationalism** and greater self-sufficiency
    - The gold standard and convertibility was abandoned
    - Currencies deprecated
    - Even Britain could no longer export more than they imported
    - People converted pounds to dollars (more secure value)
- Governments were forced to manipulate their economies in order to uphold exports
    - Exchange controls
    - Trade was bilaterally restricted, and sometimes nations resorted to bartering
    - Protective tariffs (**Smoot-Hawley tariff** of 1930 in the US decreases international trade, as other nations enact "protective" tariffs)
- 1932 **Ottawa agreements** in Britain: Britain and its dominions would have lower tariffs levied against one another
- Adoption of quotas (limits imports) and restrictions to immigration
- **International Monetary and Economic Conference** in 1933 failed to open trade around the world
    - Allies are forced to default on their payments, and Congress then denies them access to US financial markets
- **Cultural Reactions to Crisis**

- **MODERNISM** in 1920s
- Postwar decade had been an era of achievement
- Painters displayed their personal emotions and memories and experience
- Writers explored memory and the human mind
  - James Joyce- *Ulysses* (stream of consciousness)
  - Eugene O'Neill-American playwright
  - Marcel Proust- *Remembrance of Things Past*: personal and emotional experiences
  - Virginia Woolf- *To the Lighthouse*: passage of time
  - Ernest Hemingway- one of the expatriates who moved to Europe
- **REALISM** in 1930s because of Depression
- Rejected exploration of psychological anxieties as inadequate and self-indulgent
- Instead, social and political engagement: won support from intellectuals (especially those who believed in failure of capitalism)
  - Andre Gide: embraced communism and praised Soviet Union's social experiments
  - Write more about social suffering of the day (proletarian literature)
  - Malcolm Crowley-*Exile's Return*: new social problems call for new kinds of writing
  - Steinbeck-*Grapes of Wrath* (social miseries of impoverished Americans)
  - Angry political extension and cultural anxiety titled "realism"

CHAPTER 10

DEMOCRACIES & DICTATORSHIPS

Democracy and Dictatorship

- Progress was practically nonexistent, and people demanded security
- Each nation tried to become self-dependent
- There was an increased demand for security accompanied by the advancement of the welfare state and social democracy
- The Great Depression gave ambitious political leaders the opportunity to take control, whose solution to all problems was WAR!
- The United States Depression and the New Deal
- Stock market in 1929
- 1932 national income had dropped
- President Hoover did not act drastically enough to relieve people of the burdens brought upon by the Depression; he opposed immediate direct federal relief
- In 1932, Franklin Delano Roosevelt was elected
- New Deal: recovery + relief + reform
    - Program of assistance to farmers, small home owners, and industry were expanded
    - Government provided financial assistance for the relief of the unemployed and sponsored a broad public works program to employ the jobless
- "Bank holiday"- banks temporarily closed until panic subsided, and reopened under new rules
- Civilian Conservation Corps promoted conservation and reforestation, managed to employ 3 million young people
- National Recovery Administration encouraged "codes of fair competition" to help regulate prices and production
- All measures were done to create purchasing power and stimulate industrial activity
- Keynesian economics
    - Deficit financing

- o Policies of British economist John Maynard Keynes, wrote *The General Theory of Employment, Interest, and Money* (1936)
- o If private investment funds were idle, government funds must be used to encourage economic activity, so as to increase purchasing power and put more money into circulation
- o Believed **deficit spending** was the only direct and rapid method of preventing economic collapse in a capitalist system
- o Problem: how will the deficits be repaid?
- 1929: Securities and Exchange Commission was created to regulate the issuance of stock and supervise operations of stock exchange
- Tennessee Valley Authority served as a program for flood control, created more jobs
- After 1935, New Deal focused more on reform and improving the condition of labor and moderation of economic insecurity
  - o 1935 - Social Security Act - provided for unemployment, old-age, and disability insurance
  - o Fair Labor Standards Act - 40 hours was maximum work week and set minimum hourly wage, curtailed child labor
  - o National Labor Relations (Wagner) Act- provided workers the right to organize and bargain through unions, prohibited employers from interfering with union organizing or discrimination
- CIO (Congress of Industrial Organizations) came out of the AFL (American Federation of Labor)
  - o Union membership rose dramatically
- Recession did not end until 1938 when government spending resumed
- By 1929 national income rose again
- The New Deal did NOT end the depression, it ended in 1938 as armaments production increased
- The "Roosevelt Revolution" increased the role of the federal government; it began to impose controls on business and redistribute wealth
- Supreme Court declared some of his measures as unconstitutional, FDR made plans to "reorganize" the Court in an attempt to increase his power
- Roosevelt was elected to 4 terms
- New Deal represented a bold and humanitarian way of meeting the economic crisis and managed to reaffirm American faith in democracy
- British Politics: The 1920's and the Depression
- After 1914, the British began losing their markets because of the emergence of other economically aggressive industrial nations, the growth of tariff barriers and development of indigenous textile industries in the East
- British exports were suffering

- By 1921 over 2 million unemployed were receiving benefit payments called the "dole"
- The modern welfare state was well under way
- 1926: coal miners went on strike
  - Ended in failure and managed to get unions put under stricter control by Trade Disputes Act of 1927
- 1922, Labour party displaced Liberals and became the second most popular party facing the Conservatives, was committed to a policy of socialism in 1918
- Labour party did no more than extend unemployment relief and inaugurate housing a public works projects and acted firmly in the face of strikes
- Wall Street crash occurred when Labour party was in office, prime minister was Ramsay MacDonald
  - Unemployment grew
  - Gold flowed out of the country
  - Tax receipts declined
  - Public debt grew
  - MacDonald extended the dole
  - All of this outraged the Labour party
- Conservatives won election of 1924 by exploiting the Labour party as having relations with Communists
- **Britain and the Commonwealth: Imperial Relations**
  - In the Middle East, Britain controlled the Palestine mandate, with a growing trickle of European Zionists.
  - The protectorate over Egypt was ended.
  - **Irish Question**
    - In Ireland, a brief and bloody battle between the English "black and tans" and the Sinn Fein (1921-1922) resulted in the creation of the Irish Free State without Ulster in 1922, and fully independent in 1937, though it remained within the Commonwealth until 1949.
  - **The Dominions**
    - Gradually split off: The Statute of Westminster of 1931 recognized Canada, Australia, New Zealand, and South Africa as equals with each other and Great Britain--though bonds of economic cooperation remained firm.
- **France: The 1920s and the Coming of the Depression**
  - France was concerned with rebuilding and security in the 1920s, mainly under right wing parties emphasizing private enterprise and private property.
  - The "Radical Socialists", a moderate leftist party, came to power after the Ruhr crisis.

- o Antidemocratic parties on the left (communist) and right (monarchist) exerted noisy, militant pressure but had little power.
- o **Poincare's Measures**
    - Ordered the occupation of the Ruhr in 1923, balanced the budget by reduced spending and increased taxes.
    - Returning to power in 1926 he stabilized the France after a disastrous fall that virtually repudiated all internal debts--and managed to avoid catastrophic inflation.
    - Prosperity followed--tourism was important, industry was strong, but labor was unhappy.
- **Depression Ferment and the Popular Front**
    - o The Depression brought a series of unstable ministries (5 alone in 1931); government clung to retrenchment as the answer, keeping the gold standard.
    - o Fascist-type leagues grew, attacking republicanism.
    - o Right-wing Paris riots, followed by a leftist general strike, brought on a Popular Front of Socialists and Communists, enabling the victory of Leon Blum in 1936--a democratic/reformist socialist.
- **The Popular Front and After**
    - o Blum legislated the 40 hour week, wage increases, and collective bargaining, bringing huge union growth.
    - o He nationalized the arms and aviation industries, reorganized the government and reformed the Bank of France, and aided French farmers.
    - o The right called this "New Deal" a revolution, and cursed the left-wing, Socialist Jew.
    - o The reforms were long overdue, but they came at the wrong time.
    - o Nazi rearming meant France had to rearm--and France could not both reform and rearm.
    - o Employers were upset; there was a flight of gold; labor became unhappy; and the Communists were angered by the failure to aid the Spanish Loyalists in the 1936-1939 Civil War.
    - o The Popular Front came apart and Blum's government fell.
    - o The Radical Socialists under Daladier returned.
    - o Democracy had been preserved, but with cracks.
- **Western Europe and the Depression**
    - o Governments were unable to cope politically with the Depression.
    - o Old equipment, dependence on US loans, and the success of the USSR.
    - o Moreover, the birth rate bottomed out, and there was a scarcity of men in the vigorous middle years.
- **Italian Fascism**

- **Mussolini**
    - Began a leftist career as a pro-revolutionary socialist, employed as a radical journalist; in war he became a strong nationalist, believing in *Italia Irredenta.*
    - Demobilized as a corporal, he organized groups called *Fasci Italiani di Combattimento* ("Italian League of Combatants").
    - Italy had lost 600,000 dead in the war and was disappointed by Versailles; it had gained territory, but no mandates.

- **Social Unrest**
    - There was much social unrest--peasant uprisings and worker strikes, and a clear worker move towards communism.
    - Mussolini's Fascisti, dressed in black shirts, began brawling with communists in the streets.
    - The government, formed by coalitions, was weak and failed to act. In elections the fascists won 35 of the 500 seats, but got it way in the streets with its goons.
    - The propertied were thoroughly frightened of communism, and found fascist ideas comforting.
    - Mussolini had favored higher corporate taxes and attacked "war profiteering" by the rich.
    - Business support brought a shift to a "law and order", and an anti-communist program, which also appealed to nationalists and the lower middle class.
    - His squadristi (Italian: "armed squads", or *camicie nere*/black shirts) attacked strikers, unions, or any elected leftists.
    - When the left-wing called for a general strike, Mussolini called for a **"March on Rome,"** and the frightened government named Mussolini premier, with a year of full emergency powers (after a liberal cabinet had tried to pass martial law to derail Mussolini).

- **New Parliamentary Rules**
    - Mussolini now declared that the largest party would get **two-thirds** of Parliament; using control of the electoral machinery plus his **squadristi,** he won 60% of the vote in the 1924 election.

- **Matteoti's Murder**
    - A respected socialist named **Matteoti** exposed the violence by the fascists and was murdered; indignation was wide spread, but Mussolini over-rode all opposition and created a full dictatorship:
        - No parliament; censored press, no labor unions or strikes; only one party allowed--the fascists.
    - According to the fascists, democracy was weakened by class struggle and selfishness; states required a vigorous leader, Il Duce.
    - He denounced capitalism and Marxism, advocating control of the economy

by the government coordinating the activities of worker's syndicates, or the corporate state:

- All economic life was divided into 22 corporations; in each, representatives of labor, employers and the government set prices, wages, and industrial policies--with the government vote decisive, of course.

- **The corporative state**
  - **Ideology of Fascism:** Mussolini introduced the theory, the syndical or corporative state.
    - **Left wing syndicalism**
      - Looked to revolutionary labor unions to expropriate the owners of private industry
    - **Fascism/Right wing syndicalism**
      - Labor unions and private industry worked together under the guidance of government--class cooperation, not class struggle
    - Mussolini signed the Lateran accord in 1929- recognized the independence and sovereignty of Vatican City
  - Under the Fascist corporative system the authority of the state was paramount
  - 1938 the old chamber of deputies was superseded by a chamber of fasces and corporations, representing the corporations and the Fascist party.

- **The Appeal of Fascism**
  - Stability--politically and economically,
  - Recognized the need for private capital,
  - Large public works projects and military spending to stimulate the economy,
  - Full employment,
  - Nationalistic and expansionist,
  - Protection against leftists and communists

- **Opponents of Fascism**
  - The communists hated it, so did all socialists, labor leaders, moderate leftists, and idealistic democrats.

- **<u>The Nazi State</u>**
- <u>Hitler's background</u>
- Born in Austria in 1889
- Lost his father at age 14 and his mother a few years later
- Dropped out of school at 16

- Hitler didn't like what he saw in Vienna: neither the trappings of the Habsburg court, nor the nobility of Eastern Europe who rode by in their carriages, nor the mixed nationalities of the Danubian empire.
- He became violently anti-Semitic, and he also disliked aristocracy, capitalism, socialism, cosmopolitanism, internationalism and "hybridization"
- Nazi origins
- Inspired by and copied Mussolini's fascism
- Joined the German Workers Party
- In 1920 he proclaimed its 25-point program
- Monarchist and anti-republican organizations
- Used armed bands of street thugs to threaten uprisings
- Brownshirts - Hitlers private army
    - Staged the *beer hall putsch* in Munich
- *Mein Kampf* – Hitlers book of personal recollection
- The socialist nature within National Socialism lost its appeal
- The Great Depression in 1929 led to class conflict
    - Germany suffered the worst from the depression
    - It stirred up loathing for the treaty of Versailles
- Hitler's propaganda
- Hitler and Nazis inflamed above feelings with their propaganda
- Hitler called for "true" democracy
- In 1930 Nazis won 107 seats in the Reichstag
- Communist vote had risen progressively to a peak in November 1932
- In January 1933 Hitler was named chancellor of Germany
- November 9,1938: Kristallnacht
- Coordinating German Society
- Laws defined Nazi state as operating on behalf of the will of the German people
- Churches were coordinated with Nazi concepts: government encouraged anti-Christian pagan movements
- **Nazi Youth (*Hitler Jugend*)** is created
- Labor unions are legislated out of existence, replaced by **National Labor Front** (strikes are forbidden)
- **"Leadership principle"**: employers set up as small-scale Fuhrers and given extensive control, but under government supervision
- Publics works programs, rearmament program
- No more unemployment

- Although increases in labor's wages was reduced and strikes forbidden, the **Strength Through Joy** program provided workers with entertainment, vacations, and travel
- Economic autarky and self-sufficiency
- Increased control of industry, but still private ownership
- **Four Year Plan** (1936) of economic development: absolute independence from foreign trade (extreme economic nationalism)
- German chemists create artificial rubber, plastics, synthetics, other substitute products so they don't have to import raw materials
- Germany moves to dominate Eastern European trade
    - Problem with European trade: economically it works, but politically it doesn't
    - Replaces this with system of bilateral trade agreements
    - However, this new system makes Germany very powerful at the expense of everyone else
- **<u>TOTALITARIANISM – ORIGINS AND CONSEQUENCES</u>**
- <u>Soviet communism versus totalitarianism</u>
- In **<u>theory</u>**, the two were different, for the Soviets:
    - Proletariat dictatorship was temporary
    - Didn't glorify individual leader
    - Not nationalistic (emphasized worldwide class struggle)
    - Had democratic constitution
    - Not necessarily militaristic
    - Individual rights guaranteed in constitution
    - No racism
- But soon after the 1917 revolution, in the USSR:
    - One-party state became permanent
    - Hollowness of Soviet constitution and rights became apparent
    - Cult developed around Stalin
    - Exported its ideology along with conquest of others
- <u>Evolution of Totalitarianism</u>
    - Outgrowth of historical development
    - WWI sped up the process through immense demands of total war
    - 20th century totalitarian state: claimed absolute dominion over every part of state
    - State was anti-Christian, offering a whole new "philosophy" on life
- <u>Relies on historic nationalism</u>

- Rejected classical liberalism (emphasizes the individual): instead individual is only a cell of the great organism, lacking existence outside of it
- Similar to Marxism: subordination of individuals to their class
- The individual is subordinate to the party and leader: only leader can express the fundamental will of the people
- Ideas, science, and art are products of specific societies (Enlightenment ideas disappear)
- Truth is subjective and must conform to inner nature of the people, interpreted by the leader
- Propaganda
- Propaganda is vital in order to shape "reality": government manufactures thought
- Censorship becomes a necessity: manipulates opinion and rewrites history
- Ideas reflect ideology of the State, so idea of absolute truth evaporates
- People become incapable of reason
- Racism and class conflict
- Nazi racism exaggerates nationalism and national solidarity: defining nations as biological entities (same physical ancestry and physical characteristics)
- Focus on **anti-Semitism**: believes the Jews monopolize business and are inferior racially.
- Stir fears of leftist revolution,
- Claim to resolve class conflict
- Change the focus of national wealth and well-being into a Darwinian international struggle in which war is solution
- Glorification of violence
- What most distinguishes totalitarianism from democracies
- 1930s: torture reintroduced as a policy of state
- Drew from Nietzsche
- Ethics were violent and neopagan (preach direct action instead of thought)
- Youth movements appealing to juvenile idealism and stressing toughness of body
- Nazi ideologists had pseudoscientific racist theories to explain and justify actions
- **SPREAD OF DICTATORSHIP**
- No promise of restoring democracy in the future (which was the case in the 1920s)--derided by Fascists/Nazis as inefficient and the cause of economic problems
- By 1938, only 10 out of 27 European countries were democratic: Britain, France, Holland, Belgium, Switzerland, Czechoslovakia, Finland, and 3 Scandinavian countries (Denmark, Finland, Sweden)

- Contributed to collapse of representative institutions: Low education and literacy, hostile reactionary elements, fear of Bolshevism, minority dissatisfactions, and economic strains
- Most totalitarian leaders came to depend on personal and military power
- Dictators repressed individual liberties, banned opposition parties, abolished parliamentary institutions, banned strikes, anti-Semitic legislation.
- War was noble, peace was sign of weakness
- Problems blamed on foreign countries
- Cult of personality and egomaniacal leaders

CHAPTER 11
WORLD WAR II

The Pacifism and Disunity of the West

- After the devastation of WWI, French policy was defensive and sparing of man power
- French built the Maginot Line as an elaborate fortification on their eastern frontier facing Germany
    - However, France was too ideologically divided to possess any firm foreign policy
- British government tried to be noncommittal, believing in policy of appeasement
    - Chamberlain: architect of appeasement (may have been influenced by success of Luftwaffe in Guernica)
- *Cordon sanitaire* - a policy of containment created in 1919; ring of small states on the border of USSR who opposed Bolshevism and were anti-soviet
- Soviets became interested in collective security; joined League of Nations in 1934
- The March of Nazi and Fascist Aggression
- Adolf Hitler employed tactics that played on the hopes for peace and fears of war of democratic peoples
- 1933: took Germany out of the League and Disarmament Conference
    - 1934: Germany signs nonaggression treaty with Poland
    - Hitler demands union of Austria and Germany
    - 1936: Hitler repudiated the Locarno agreements and reoccupied the Rhineland
        - French government was divided and unwilling to act without Britain. However, the British didn't want to risk another war.
    - 1938: German forces move into Austria and the two are unified by force of arms
- 1935: Italy invaded Ethiopia, depose Haile Selassie; League fails to prevent this
- Rome-Berlin Axis: Mussolini and Hitler came to an agreement in 1936

- Japan and Germany signed Anti-Comintern pact (Italy would sign too)- agreement to oppose communism (1936)
    - Meanwhile, 1937 Japan invades China and occupied the capital; the West was too distracted in Europe to prevent Japan from overrunning Asia

- **The Spanish Civil War, 1936-1939**

- 1931: establishment of the democratic Spanish Republic

- Soon after anticlerical legislation was enacted

- Attempted to break up some of the larger landed estates and redistribute the land

- 1936, new elections were held, a leftist groups joined a Popular Front, won victory at the polls. Country is polarized by swing left in parliament
    - General Francisco Franco emerged as the leader of the center-right Nationalist forces
    - Parties of the right united in resistance against the Republican government (600,000 people died)

- Britain and France forbade shipment of war materials to Spain, they wanted to stay out of any war

- However, Germany and Italy support Franco/Nationalists and denounce republican government), and the Soviet Union supports the Republicans

- Spain becomes a geopolitical contest between the forces of fascism and communism
    - Picasso's *Guernica* (1937) was a representation of fascist bombing civilian centers during Spanish Civil War

- Nazi-Soviet Pact of 1939 spells the end of USSR involvement in Spain

- Franco wins, although a fascist, he will keep Spain neutral during WWII and will give safe haven to Jews

- **The Munich Crisis: Climax of Appeasement**

- Czechoslovakia, Romania and Yugoslavia formed the Little Entente

- Czechs accept British mediation on Sudetenland since Hitler was planning to invade in 1938

- Hitler invited Chamberlain and Daladier (French premier) and Mussolini to a conference in Munich; Chamberlain and Daladier urge Czechoslovakia to yield to Hitler's terms; they did

- Chamberlain claimed he had brought "peace to our time", yet this was temporary and emboldened Hitler

- 1939, Hitler declared Slovakia independent, took Memel from Lithuania and demanded Danzig and the Polish Corridor; Mussolini took over Albania

- Soviets decide to sign nonaggression treaty with Nazi Germany in 1939
    - Agreed to divide Poland between them
    - Soviets would enjoy influence in the Baltic states

- o Soviets would stay out of any wars between Germany and Poland or Western states
- Germans invaded Poland on September 1st, 1939; two days later Great Britain and France declared war on Germany
- **The Years of Axis Triumph**
- **German Blitzkrieg**
  - o Hitler buried Poland in a one-month blitzkrieg; 3 weeks after the Germans start their attack the USSR moved in to take eastern Poland and the Baltic republics.
  - o Finland resisted Soviet demands and the result was war in November, with the USSR expelled from the League. USSR wins, but only after heavy losses (the generals of the German Wehrmacht notice Russian military inefficiency).
- **The "Phony War"**
  - o Lack of military action in the West was termed the Phony War: Allied and Axis troops faced each other across the Maginot and Siegfried Lines.
  - o But the Blitzkrieg resumed in April. Denmark fell in hours, followed several weeks later by Norway.
  - o The **Wehrmacht** then sped through the Low Countries and into France, successfully completing the WWI Schlieffen Plan and cutting off the British forces--which were evacuated in the "Miracle of Dunkirk".
- **Vichy France**
  - o Having lacked armor, an air force, or unity, France signed an armistice on June 22nd
  - o Northern France was occupied, with Vichy France in the south under collaborationist forces led by General Petain (a hero of WWI).
  - o Italy also attacked southern France--and later Greece and north Africa.
  - o Germany proceeded to create a "New Order" in the style of Napoleon, running western Europe to coordinate and exploit resources, industry, and labor.
- **American Aid**
  - o Only Britain held out, under Churchill--who immediately sought US help.
  - o Interventionists wanted war to destroy fascism, but isolationism remained strong.
  - o FDR amended the Neutrality Acts allowing the US to become the "arsenal of democracy" to secure the Four Freedoms.
  - o He made the Destroyer-Base deal (an executive agreement, not requiring Congressional approval) in 1940.
    - ▪ 50 over-age destroyers in exchange for US use of British
      - Caribbean bases
    - ▪ Lend-Lease in 1941.

- All on the premise that it was only neighborly to loan Britain the means to keep fighting to stop fascism.
  - The US began to build an army with conscription.
  - The US occupied bases in Greenland and Iceland to ease the problems of Britain in securing its lifeline to the West.
  - Britain soon faced the "**Battle of Britain**", with German bombing raids -- but the RAF controlled the air: use of radar and information provided due to the breaking of the German secret codes.
  - Britain was disrupted, but far from defeated.

- **The Russian Front**
  - Meanwhile, there was an uneasy peace in the East, with the Germans upset over Russia's moves into the Baltic and Balkans.
  - By 1941, Hitler had made alliances with Rumania, Bulgaria, and Hungary; his goal was to take over the Ukraine.
  - He began the war with a sudden blitzkrieg on June 22, quickly besieging Leningrad and moving on Sebastopol in the Crimea and on Moscow.
  - Russian resistance proved stubborn; the attack had been delayed a month while Hitler cleaned up Mussolini's mess in Greece and took Crete from Britain.
  - The delay, plus an early winter, aided the Soviets in defeating the Nazi assault in a counterattack.
  - In 1942 Hitler renewed his attack, taking the Crimea and moving on Stalingrad, while continuing the attack on Moscow and besieging Leningrad.
  - Division of forces, in combination with the Soviet "scorched earth" policy and the growing partisan resistance behind the lines, ultimately made possible a stalemate that in 1943. By 1944 German retreat was turned into a rout.
  - Another important reason for failure was the German treatment of Russians as *untermenschen* (subhuman). Although at first hailed as liberators from Stalin's rule, once the population saw they were being mistreated more by the Nazis, they turned against them.

- **Other Military Campaigns**
  - Hitler sent Rommel into North Africa to rescue the Italian forces; Rommel then launched an attack to attempt to take the Suez Canal in late 1942.
  - The British had thrashed the Italians, both in East Africa (Ethiopia and Somaliland) and in Libya, but Rommel's *Afrika Korps* pushed the British back close to Alexandria.
  - At the same time, the Japanese had launched their attack on the Allies, catching the US unprepared at Pearl Harbor and in the Philippines, and rapidly sweeping through British, French, and Dutch colonial possessions.
  - The attack was a reaction to the US move to embargo oil and scrap metal for Japan; without these vital raw materials Japanese expansionist aims

would have been thwarted.

- o In the Atlantic, German U-boats were at their peak and sinking incredible tonnage of Allied shipping. Thus 1942 was the Allied nadir.

- **THE ALLIED OFFENSIVE**

- The eastern front

  - o 1944 – Russians pushed the Germans out of Ukraine, Byelorussia, Baltic states, and Poland

  - o Underground Polish uprising against Germans in Warsaw, but Soviets do not want Poland to be liberated by noncommunist Polish leadership, so they permit Germans to crush uprising

  - o Next, the Russians push southward into Romania and Bulgaria, and these countries switched sides and declared war on Germany

  - o Early 1945: Soviets reopen their offensive into the West: reach **Oder**, 40 miles from Germany!

- Final drive on Germany

  - o Hitler switches military focus from west to Oder

  - o Americans reach the Elbe, but Eisenhower halts them there (already overextended, want clear line of demarcation from USSR, and afraid of final German stand in Alps), and to preserve the good will with Soviets (acknowledge their heavy losses, and maintain Western-Soviet coalition) – they permit them to take Berlin

  - o Soviets also allowed to take Czech capital

  - o Soviets are now in control of all major capitals in central and eastern Europe

    - Allies and Soviets demanded unconditional surrender, and Germans kept fighting in Berlin!

  - o Hitler commits suicide

    - **Admiral Doenitz** named his successor, he surrenders on May 8, 1945

    - The war in Europe is over!

- Only now did the Allies become fully aware of the Nazi horrors of WWII

- Hostages and villages killed for resistance, concentration camps (**Auschwitz** 12,000 killed per day)

  - o People who were "inferior" were liquidated

    - At first, used firing squads and carbon monoxide from autos used to kill "undesirables", but death camps become more sophisticated: some worked to death, others killed at once.

      - 6 million Jews killed

      - Others killed included Poles, Russians, Slavic peoples, and Gypsies

        - o This was the **"final solution"**

- The reason why Hitler's **Holocaust** was so terrible: it was a modern genocide of massive scale, with intentional, state-sponsored and scientific organization

- <u>War in the Pacific</u>
- Series of attacks on islands (**island hopping**) to weaken Japanese navy and naval air force as the U.S. slowly makes its way to Japan
- Japan's industry and navy were shattered, but Allies insisted on unconditional surrender
- Allies prepared a full-scale invasion; because they didn't believe Japan would surrender
- Bombing of **Hiroshima and Nagasaki**
- USSR declares war on Japan and invades Manchuria
- Japan surrenders: the emperor is allowed to remain, but there is occupation by the US army
- **<u>FOUNDATIONS OF THE COMING PEACE</u>**
- No clear-cut peace settlement, instead terms gradually emerged
- **Atlantic Charter** (1941; ideological basis for peace) set the US and British goals (similar to 14 Points) – sovereign rights of nations, equal access to world trade, increased security
- **Casablanca Conference** 1943: unconditional surrender was set as the goal, to avoid ambiguity of 1918
- **Tehran Conference** 1943: first meeting of Roosevelt, Churchill, and Stalin (**Big Three**: US, USSR, Britain)
  - Plans for occupation and demilitarization of postwar Germany, and an international organization which will be the United Nations
  - FDR wanted to preserve unity, so avoided tough decisions
  - Churchill was more anxious to get key promises from Stalin
  - The West pledged Normandy invasion ASAP and USSR pledged offensive on Eastern front
  - No political agreements made
  - Result: USSR has hegemony over eastern Europe
- **<u>Yalta Agreements 1945</u>**
    - Most important wartime conference: at this point, Allies are close to victory
    - **Declaration on Liberated Europe**: Stalin promises free elections to provide representative, provisional governments (will violate all promises)
    - USSR would get half of the reparations from Germany; other half would go to countries that had borne main burden of the war
    - Russian-Polish boundary to be at **Curzon Line**

- Poles are compensated at the expense of Germans
- Germany to be disarmed and divided into 4 occupation zones (Big Three + France)
- USSR will enter war with Japan within 3 months of defeat of Germany in exchange for lands lost to Japan in Russo-Japanese War of 1905
- International organization (UN) would be created

- **United Nations**
- International mandate to preserve future peace and security
- Made up of **Security Council** (of Great Powers: have veto power) and **General Assembly** - dispute over how many votes USSR would get
- FDR wanted concessions from USSR to defeat Japan and produce postwar harmony, but Churchill was more anxious for specific political divisions, with spheres of influence for each power

- **Potsdam Conference 1945**
- **Truman** (FDR had died), **Atlee** (Churchill defeated in elections), and Stalin
- Deepening disagreements over Europe questions, German reparations, etc.
  - Agreed on postwar disarmament, deNazification, demilitarization
  - Nations get reparations from Germany in their own occupation zones
- Russia gains territory in West, so Poland also expands westward
- Russian areas of Poland in east were returned
- Germany divided between USSR (north) and Poland (south
- Many Germans driven from Poland and Sudetenland, have to go back to Germany
- Other agreements
- Other peace treaties signed in 1947 with Italy, Romania, Hungary, Bulgaria, Finland: all paying reparations and agreeing to territorial settlements (favoring USSR)
- 1951: western Allies made peace with Japan without participation of USSR (Soviets made separate treaty in 1956)
- No final agreement ever concluded on Germany
- Western-Soviet coalition fell apart after war; results in new age of crisis

Dr. Juan R. Céspedes, Ph.D.

CHAPTER 12
THE COLD WAR & RECONSTRUCTION

Occupation of Japan

- In China the Chinese Communists triumphed over the Nationalists and Mao Zedong proclaimed the People's Republic of China an 1949.

- Japan—US used military occupation from 1945 to 1952 to foster parliamentary institutions and review the Japanese economy.

- US didn't want Soviet to share occupation of Japan, so with UK and France's support, General Douglas MacArthur became supreme commander of the occupation forces.

- American occupation encouraged economic revival and political reconstruction.

- 1946: new constitution ended divine rule by emperor, transferred sovereignty from the emperor to the people, established machinery for parliamentary government, gave women the vote, and encouraged local self-government.

  o It forever renounced war and the threat or use of force as a means of settling international disputes; the small Japanese armed forces were to be restricted to defensive purposes.

  o The Japanese paid reparations to Asian nations that had been the victims of Japanese conquest.

- Efforts at social and economic reform were less sweeping than originally planned.

- **Economic Recovery**

- Japanese cooperated with American occupation forces in order to restore Japan (were relieved that the Americans were not going to be vindictive).

- Emperor received special status so he was shielded from blame regarding the war

- Large family holdings were dissolved and broken up

- Labor unions were reinstated, but their power was weakened

- Small farmers lacked capital to buy pieces of broken up land holdings

- Socialist party emerged and people expressed discontent but conservatives still controlled the government

- Conservatives were committed to the economic recovery of Japan

  o By 1954 their GNP was restored to prewar levels

- o Social unrest was kept to a minimum due to labor self-discipline and social deference
- Cooperation between government and businesses encouraged investment and economic growth
- 1950's: economy grew at 10% per year, manufacturing grew at 14%
- Japan still had a labor shortage so they compensated for this by engaging in automation to speed up production
- Japan quickly became notable for their technologic innovations, with consumer products entering the world economy
- Because there was no large military, all government expenditures were reinvested into industry
- Japan quickly became an integral part of the world economy
- **Containment in Asia: The Korean War**
- **East Asia in 1950**
- Key Allies and Soviets agreed that Korea would be free after Japan was defeated, but in 1945 the US suggested the Soviets occupy Korea
- USSR ends up establishing satellite government under the control of Kim Il Sung and built up military strength in North Korea
- US took control of the South
- First sign of trouble: 1947 the UN sought to sponsor nationwide elections, but the Soviets would not permit them in the North
- Two Koreas came into existence unintentionally
- By 1950, Japan was revived, very friendly with the West
- USSR and China allied out of mutual concern for the revival of Japan and the growth of America influence in eastern Asia
- June 1950: Korean war broke out: North Korea invades South Korea (communists concerned that the two would unite on pro-Western terms)
  - o Soviets helped the North Korean army prepare for invasion; checked American influence in Asia
  - o US was denounced by communists and their allies for intervening in Asia
- **A Test of Wills**
- Truman, who saw this as a test of the "free world's commitment to liberty," used the UN as a "police force" to send combat troops and air-strikes to North Korea at the 38th parallel; MacArthur was in charge of UN multinational forces
- MacArthur's threats to the Chinese could escalate to a full-scale war; fires him due to public support of not wanting another war
- **Cease-fire and Armistice**
- 1951: cease-fire agreement
- 1953: armistice was signed, partition was agreed at the 38th parallel, with agreement of demilitarized buffer zone

- North Korea = communist under Kim Il Sung
- South Korea = capitalist economy, 40,000 American troops remained to protect buffer zone, very difficult to achieve democracy under the elected autocrat Syngman Rhee
- **Results of the Korean War**
- US spent $15 billion on the war
- Although 15 countries participated in the war, US was major player
    - 54,000 American battle deaths
- Show of American firmness in foreign policy was reassuring
- **American Involvement in Asia**
- Korean war inaugurated extensive American involvement in Asia
- 1952: US tested H-bomb
- 1953: Soviets tested H-bomb
- Americans press for rearmament of West Germany
- West Germany authorized to create an army under command of NATO after 1954
- 1955: Federal Republic of Germany became a member of NATO
- **Peace with Japan**
- Korean War hastened a formal peace treaty with Japan.
- Treaty was signed in 1951 in San Francisco by 50 nations (except USSR)
- No general reparations
- Individual countries would work out their own reparation agreements
- U.S. retained military rights in Japan and occupied nearby islands until there was peace and security.
- 1952 = U.S. occupation of Japan ended
- U.S. signed security pacts with Australia, New Zealand, and Philippines
- Decades following troubled international relations of early Cold War :
    - Crises over Berlin, Cuba, Vietnam, Middle East, Africa
    - Mounting nuclear arms race between two superpowers
    - Stockpiling of formidable weapons
- **WESTERN EUROPE: ECONOMIC RECONSTRUCTION**
- *The Marshall Plan and European Recovery*
- **U.S. Economic Strength**
- Single most important factor in the early post war years was the **productivity of the American economic system.**
- American economy had expanded enormously during WWII.
    - United States accounted for 2/3 of the world's industrial production.
    - United States held 2/3 of the world's gold.

- o U.S. gross national product was 2.5 times higher than in 1939.
- o U.S. exports were 3 times greater.
- By 1947, the economies of Western Europe were approaching prewar levels of production.
- American aid was needed, though, to continue to buy food, fuel, raw materials, and industrial parts needed for recovery.
- Spring 1947 increased tension since Western Europe experienced the poorest harvest.
- Americans became concerned with western European stability.
- Soviets had more to gain by chaos in Western Europe and the United States had more to gain by rebuilding.
- **The Marshall Plan** (also called the European Recovery Program)
- Thus far, American economic aid had been improvised and piecemeal.
- The Marshall Plan was developed by Secretary of State George C. Marshall, and enacted by Congress
  - o The plan was "directed not against country or doctrine, but against hunger, poverty, desperation, and chaos."
- U.S. extended the invitation to all European governments including the USSR and Eastern European states.
- Soviet Union rejected this proposal, and forbade the participation of its East European satellites.
- Eager response from Western European countries.
- American aid was coordinated with each country's needs and with joint European priorities to maximize benefits.
- The Office for European Economic Cooperation (OEEC) in Paris, worked closely with Americans and identified projects, coordinated the planning, and allocated the funds.
- **Results of the Marshall Plan**
- Western Europeans improved transportation facilities, modernized their infrastructure, and expanded their productive capacity
- Reduced trade barriers
- Hard currency reduced financial pressures
- Cemented W. European loyalties to the US
  - o Blocked influence of communist parties in W. Europe
  - o Helped fuel the postwar boom in the US
- *Economic Growth in Western Europe*
- **The Silver '50s and Golden '60s**
- By 1958 Fed. Rep. of Germany became the leading industrial country of west Europe

- European economies were growing at unprecedented rates of growth (1948 to 1974)
- **Economic Planning and Government Intervention**
  - Prosperity was due to economic planning, social services, and government intervention
  - Full employment = GOAL
- GB, GR, Italy - postwar governments nationalized key sectors of the economy
- Even in these mixed economies the private sector was still major part of the economy
- **A Steady Stream of Immigrants**
- By 1958 West Germany was the leading industrial country of western Europe
- 1948 to 1974 were years of tremendous economic growth in Europe
- Britain lagged economically
  - It had older factories, more competition, and difficulty with colonial territories
- Keynes's theories were employed to smooth the economic swings
- Some steps toward nationalizing industry led to mixed economies in Europe
- Labor shortages led to immigration from
  - Turkey
  - North Africa
  - Indonesia
  - India
  - Pakistan
  - West Africa
- Cultural unrest began to emerge cultural clashes
- Welfare state grew to meet the demands for social benefits, but burdened economic growth
- By the 1970s questions began to emerge about the entitlements and their potential as an impediment to economic growth
- Challenges for the west at the end of the war
- Britain was economically exhausted (first felt economic/military strain when providing aid to Monarchists during the Greek Civil War)
- Liquidating its empire
- France was engaged in colonial wars
  - Algiers
  - Indochina
- Germany was divided and under military occupation
- Dictatorships faded, except in the Americas and other developing countries

- **Growth of the Welfare State**
- WESTERN EUROPE: POLITICAL RECONSTRUCTION
- *Great Britain: Labor and Conservative*
- **Labor Government**
- July 1945 election in England unseated Winston Churchill
- Clement Attlee was Prime Minister
- Government change: from capitalism to parliamentary socialism and welfare state.
- Bank of England is Nationalized
- 4/5 of industry was in private hands = Mixed Economy (Capitalism and Socialism)
- Social Insurance Program was revamped
- Beveridge Report of 1942: Guarantees full employment in a free society
- Comprehensive National Health Service established
- Election of 1951: Labor Party loses majority in Parliament and Conservatives regain power.
- **A Modest Prosperity**
- Conservatives (during their control of Parliament 1951-1964) restore to private control industries that had been nationalized; modify national health insurance program; did little else to dismantle welfare state
- **Both parties realize a prosperous economy is needed to support welfare state**
- Britain weaker after WWII than after WWI
- Pound undermined by:
    - Liquidation of investments to pay for war
    - Loss of export markets
    - Reduced income from shipping and other services
- Economy improves to modest prosperity because of:
- American financial aide
- Intensified export trade
- Austerity program that reduced government spending on welfare programs
- Curtailment of military and imperial commitments
- BUT, Britain failed (for now, anyway) to rebuild their obsolescent capital equipment and infrastructure as effectively as other western European countries
- British economy growing slower than Japanese and other western European economies
- Labour says Conservatives lack "economic dynamism" (dynamism = vigorous economic activity and progress), so they're responsible for lagging economy
- However, Labour in power did not do better; had to devalue pound, extend austerity measures

- Inflation in late '60s, intensifies in '70s, unions demand wage increases
- Strikes, work stoppages troubled economy, divided British society
- Until late '70s, the question was whether Labour or the Conservatives could better manage British decline, not how they could overcome it
- **Troubles in Northern Ireland**
- After partition in 1922, 6 counties of Northern Ireland (mostly Protestant) remain part of UK
- Catholic minority (1/3 of pop.) protests and presses for annexation to Republic of Ireland
- 1969: Open violence breaks out, inflamed by Irish Republican Army (IRA) on one side and Protestant extremists on the other
  - 3,000 killed by this sectarian violence
  - At end of century, compromise in sight, buy serious problems persisted
- **The Cold War: The Opening Decade, 1945-1955**
- Science (atomic bomb and soon the hydrogen bomb), organization of industrial society (US vs USSR) and national sovereignty (UN) now represent more complex and problems then ever.
- **The Atomic Bomb**
- Science transformed both industry and war
- The atomic bomb dramatized the problem of science because people were terrified of its effects as seen through Nagasaki and Hiroshima
- People have always known that science would bring great innovations (such as vaccines) and great dangers (nuclear warfare); science could be constructive or destructive.
- It was the magnitude of destructive possibilities that caused worries
- More powerful nuclear weapons made the idea of a third WW unthinkable, since the annihilation of civilization and mankind was possible: shocking thought especially for a society that had placed one of its highest values on scientific progress
  - Opposing thesis: science is neutral and cannot be blamed for the horrors of Nagasaki and Hiroshima, the governments who used the weapons are to blame
- **Organizing Industrial Society**
- Problem of organizing industrial society was unresolved after 1945
- In theory two opposite social poles: Another postwar question was about the unity of the modern world
- There developed a more tightly knit interdependent economy that was affected by global environmental changes, interacting cultures and religions
- Far from homogeneous. However No one wanted to be subordinated, and no one wanted to be governed by an international body (national sovereignty)
- **The United Nations**

- Founded in San Francisco in 1945
- Designed to maintain international peace and security and to encourage cooperative solutions to international economic, and cultural problems
- All states, regardless of size would be represented
- General Assembly- any country could be apart of this
- All member states had an equal vote
    - o Security council
    - o Preservation of peace intended goal
- Five Great Powers: permanent members of the Security Council (US, USSR, China, Britain, France)
    - o 10 rotating members chosen for two year terms
    - o Each superpower had veto power
    - o Could not do anything unless Great Powers were unanimous
- UN 51 members originally; 189 by 2000
- Headquarters in New York
- Declaration of Human Rights was signed, but with no means to enforce (1948, principally because of Eleanor Roosevelt)
- UN significance
- Couldn't lessen or stop ideological and geopolitical differences between US and Soviet Union
- However, helped mediate regional disputes and with peacekeeping missions
- UN expanded and included third world countries (developing nations/former colonies)
- General Assembly serves as a forum for airing disputes
- **The Cold War: Origins and Nature**
- Post WWII, only US and USSR are left as world superpowers
    - o US- physically unscathed with stronger economy than ever, possessed atomic bomb
    - o USSR- still a military power despite losses, recaptured territory as Red Army advanced across Eastern Europe
    - o Both continental land giants with abundant resources.
- Development of a 2 state system, with each power knowing in advance its main adversary
    - o Difficult to establish diplomatic equilibrium.
    - o Every action taken by the other exaggerated and seen as act of aggression or provocation
    - o Ideological tension between capitalist democracy and Marxist-Leninist state (commonly referred to as "communist")
    - o "Cold War" a widening diplomatic, geopolitical and ideological clash of

interests.

- o Always fell short of direct military hostilities
- **Containment**
- Regardless of Soviet motives, Truman and the American public generally believed Soviets wanted to expand communism globally.
- US saw responsibility to "contain" this offensive, and blamed most international problems on Kremlin
- Soviet armies occupied eastern Europe and Germany to Elbe River after war; US, GB, and French Armies occupy rest of Germany, most of Austria, all Italy
- Whoever liberated a given area had political authority there: differences in rule
  - o Soviets had political domination over most of eastern/central Europe
  - o Other excluded Soviets from occupation of Italy and in Japan.
  - o USSR interpreted control as full economic, political and social control and right to shape them in own image
- Western powers sought to establish democratic societies that would become open trade partners
- US and GB had allowed Soviet dominance in east during war, but now resented it.
- **Concerns About Soviet Expansion**
- For the Soviets occupation meant full control over the political, economic and social institution of countries and the right to shape them in its own image
  - o Private property banned
  - o Collectivization of all industry
  - o State control of all media
  - o Communist one party state
  - o Ideological loyalty to Marxist principles demanded
  - o State mandated atheism
- Stalin believed this kind of transformation was the only way to guarantee "friendly regimes" on his borders
- For the Americans, Soviet control over eastern Europe seemed like the first step in a plan for unlimited expansion in Europe and elsewhere (not unlike the Nazis and fascists)
- A series of Soviet actions fed the belief that Stalin's ambitions transcended eastern Europe:
  - o Soviets had declared war on Japan in August 1945 and moved into Manchuria where they were to help the Chinese Communists
  - o The Soviets supported communist insurgents during the Greek Civil War (1946-1949)
  - o In Korea, the Soviets occupied the Northern part of the country and transformed their occupation zone into a Communist government

- o Supported Mao during in his struggle against Chiang
- Soviets also sought a trusteeship over the former Italian colonies in North Africa, pressing for joint control over the Black Sea straights and for naval access to the Mediterranean through the Dardanelles
- The Communist pressures on Turkey, Greece, and Iran aroused deep British and American concerns about Soviet strategic designs on the eastern Mediterranean and on the oil reserves of the Middle East (failed to evacuate troops in Iran)
- **Mutual Mistrust**
- Tensions- plan for international supervision of nuclear weapons
  - o U.S proposed in 1946 that atomic energy be controlled by an international authority and that its use be limited to peaceful purposes
  - o International body would have the right to send inspectors into any country to check violations and enforce sanctions that would not be subject to veto in the Security Council
  - o **Soviets objected**
  - o The British were fearful of an American relapse into isolationism and undertook to become a nuclear power of their own
  - o Soviets proceeded with their own atomic bomb research
  - o 1949- Soviets tested atomic bomb. Nuclear arms race began
- Political Conflicts:
  - o American policy of containment postulated that the Russians would expand wherever a power vacuum existed
  - o West needed to maintain its military strength and use economic and other counter pressures to resist the Soviets
  - o Churchill makes a speech on March 1949 in which he described the "iron curtain" that had descended between eastern and western Europe
- **The Truman Doctrine**
- 1947- GB can no longer aid the anti-Communist forces in Greece or support Turkey, which is under communist pressures
- Truman agrees to provide the necessary assistance in the Mediterranean
- 1947- formulates a broad national policy to contain communism everywhere
- Truman Doctrine- committed the U.S to unprecedented involvement in global military and economic affairs
- The Marshall Plan 1947- designed to hasten European economic recovery and check Communist expansion
- National Security Council and CIA created
- **Soviet Suspicions**
- Denounced America as capitalist and imperialist "war mongers"
- Stated in propaganda that it felt threatened and encircled because Americans:

- o Possessed the atomic bomb soon after WWII
- o Armed forces in occupation of Japan, Okinawa, and South Korea
- Reestablished the Comintern, renaming it the Cominform (1947)
- A serious crisis arose over Berlin after the Czech Communist party seized power in 1948
- **Germany: The Berlin Blockade and the Airlift of 1948-1949**
- Germany's consequences
    - o Germany was divided by Allied agreement into four zones and occupied by the United States, the Soviet Union, Britain, and France. Each of the four powers occupied its own zone.
    - o Berlin was also divided into four separate Allied sectors, but they were jointly administrated.
    - o The portion of Germany occupied by the Soviets was required to pay reparations, in both capital equipment and current production mainly to the USSR. Limits were also placed on German productive capacity.
- *Germany: The Berlin Blockade and the Airlift of 1948-1949*
- **Two Germanys Emerge**
- Economic reconstruction of West Germany to accelerate European recovery and to reduce European dependence on American financial aid. (U.S. & Britain)
- Ruhr was Europe's industrial heartland
- Soviets were determined to use East German resources to repair their own country. Confiscated food and machinery from their zone… Western Allies disallowed them to take their share of production from any other zone.
- Bizonia: United States and Britain united their two zones (1947) and soon after, the French united with US and GB as well.
    - o Western powers encouraged reconstruction of governments in the individual German states and the convening of a constituent assembly to set up a federal republic.
    - o Soviets created a Communist-dominated government.
- **Berlin Blockade and Airlift**
- The Atlantic Alliance
- Berlin Blockade Airlift
    - o June 1948
    - o Soviets were not consulted about the wartime agreement to treat Germany as an political/economic unit (with its own currency) so they blockaded all road and rail access to Berlin
    - o Allies organize a massive air lift.
    - o For almost a year, American and Western aircraft flew in thousands of tons of food and other supplies to the occupation forces and to the inhabitants of west Berlin.

- May of 1949- Blockade by USSR lifted.
- Each side had a different formation of German government.
    - Federal Republic of Germany
    - The German Democratic Republic
- **The Atlantic Alliance**
- **NATO**
- Stands for North Atlantic Treaty Organization
    - Network of military arrangements and a chain of command led by General Eisenhower (later becomes POTUS).
    - Large numbers of American troops were stationed in W. Berlin as the nucleus of the NATO armed forces.
    - NATO defense strategy was based primarily on American airpower rather than on ground troops alone.
- With Marshall Plan, Western Europe was making impressive economic recovery and cooperated with each other.
- To compete against US' growing power and alliances, the Soviet Union drew 6 satellite states closer economically and formed in 1949 a Council for Mutual Economic Aid to formalize economic ties (COMECON).
    - Military alliances in 1955 with Warsaw Pact
- **Purging Collaborators in France**
- After the liberation of France, General Charles de Gaulle became president.
- Elections were held for a Constituent Assembly
    - Rightist parties= discredited
    - Leftist parties= prestige
- Communists, Socialists, and Popular Republican Party (MRP) (Catholic Progressive Party) formed a provisional government
    - Expelled from cabinet in May 1947
- Left wanted a purge of collaborators
    - Began when army reached French soil
    - Drumhead trials and executions
- Fourth Republic
    - Presidency was only ceremonial
    - Cabinet = responsible to National Assembly
- Charles de Gaulle
    - Didn't like:
        - Constitution of 1946
        - Return of rivalry parties
        - Dominant role of the legislature

- o He believed that a dominant role of legislature interfered with his vision of a strong France
    - ▪ Resigned in 1946
- **"Rally of the French People"**
- Parliamentary division and ministerial instability became more severe
    - o MRP and socialists formed unstable coalitions
- De Gaule returned to the political scene
    - o Headed the "Rally for the French People"
        - ▪ "Above" other parties
- Fourth Republic
    - o Unstable; 25 cabinets from 1946-1958
    - o Social security = expanded
- Jean Monnet
    - o Economic plan
        - ▪ Paved the way for industrial expansion
        - ▪ Government, management, and labor, played mutual roles
        - ▪ Production
        - ▪ Industrial output
- **French Colonial Wars**
- Brought down the Fourth Republic
    - o Trying to preserve the old French colonial empire.
    - o Was continuously at war, for about 15 years, fighting wars in Vietnam and then Algeria.
- Constitution of 1946
    - o Provided representation in Paris for the colonies.
        - ▪ Limited reforms.
        - ▪ Didn't satisfy nationalist desires.
- 1946-1954
    - o French forces fought unsuccessfully in Indochina against the independence movements.
    - o French withdrew.
    - o The Algerian war broke out.
    - o Drained resources, moral and self-esteem of the French.
    - o European settlers and army leaders opposed French withdrawal.
    - o Staged an insurrectionary coup in Algiers May 1958.
    - o Civil war threatened the country (Algeria).
- Charles de Gaulle

- o Believed to be able to save the situation; WWII icon to the French.
- o At first promised that he would keep Algeria French.
- o Army leaders, settlers in Algeria, and parties of the Right supported him.
- o In 1958, the National Assemble invested him as a premier.
  - Gave him the authority to prepare a new constitution.

- Fifth Republic
  - o 1958
  - o Accepted by the popular referendum
  - o Gaulle was elected president.
  - o The president was the final authority in foreign affairs, and national defense.
  - o Was named prime minister and had the right to dissolve the National Assembly, call for new elections, and assume emergency of powers.
  - o Political instability disappeared.
  - o In the first 11 years of the Fifth Republic there were only three cabinets.

- **May 1968**
- Situation: restless France, reorganized Socialist party, skepticism about de Gaulle's foreign involvement.
- Suddenly in May 1968:
  - o Overcrowded universities-student revolts and demonstrations
- 10 million workers on strike
- Although this paralyzed the economy and threatened the regime, de Gaulle came out ahead in elections by securing army support.

- **The Federal Republic of Germany**
- **The Nuremberg Trials**
- The 4 wartime allies convened international trials at Nuremberg, Germany, during '45-'46 concerning Nazi war crimes
- 22 Nazi leader were indicted for "waging a war of aggression" and "crimes against humanity"
- Evidence OF mass genocide and other evil deeds was recorded
- Despite their high moral purpose, some critics disputed the validity of the trials (victors trying the ß).
- However the trials were a milestone on determining standards of civilized behavior. Only 3 of the Nazi leaders were he nazi leaders were acquitted.

- **Denazification**
- Carried out by the 4 occupation authorities
- Difficult to carry out since so many professional and technically trained Germans had been members of the Nazis

- Most evil still being captured and tried decades later (although not at Nuremberg)
- Only at end of century did victims or victim's families receive some financial restitution
- **A "Social Market Economy"**
- West German government encouraged private industry and capitalism
- Also provided broad social services
  - Therefore "social market economy"
- "Codetermination" law
  - Gave workers seats on the boards of directors of larger firms
- Constitutional Convention in Bonn 1948 with 10 German states
- Produced Basic Law (Grundgesetz)
  - Basic constitution until Germany could be united
- **The Power of the Chancellor**
- Voted indirectly (not popular vote)
- Figurehead but head of government
- Exercise moral authority
- Bundestag
- Popularly elected lower house
- Proportional representation for parties
- Party only received seats if more than 5% of vote
- 2 chief parties emerged
  - Christian Democratic Union
  - Social Democrats
- **The European Community/Common Market**
- In 1967 three communities consolidated themselves into the European Community.
  - Members took seats by party affiliation not by nation.
  - Met in Strasbourg
- In 1979 they were chosen by means of election through a European wide electorate.
- Final decision-making rested with the council of ministers whose decisions on important matters were unanimous.
  - Predecessor to European Union (EU)
- Great Britain refrained from joining the Common Market
- In 1960, Britain helped create a more limited customs union of seven states to reduce tariff barriers.
  - It was somewhat successful but it was nothing compared to the Common Market.

- De Gaulle regarded Britain and its "special relationship" with the United States as a threat to French leadership on the Continent.

- **Advance Toward Political Unity**

- De Gaulle opposed political or supranational authority for the Community.

- The common supranational economic and political machinery of the European civil servants was a favorable signs for future unity, even apart from the military and defense ties that brought the Western Europeans together in NATO.

- The likelihood of complete political union remained remote.

- Europeans showed no haste to surrender their national sovereignty and independence.

- The European Community created a strong sense of common destiny, a shared faith in democratic institutions and market economies and a concern for human rights and social needs.

- By the beginning of the twenty-first century, the European Community was projecting its own transitional military force.

- **West European Competition**

- Western Europe accounted in the 1960s for ¼ of all imports and 1/5 of exports in the world economy.

- 1/3 of the largest multinational corporations which set up subsidiaries outside their own country were European.

- London, Frankfurt, and Paris were important financial centers.

- In 1971, Western European steel production surpassed that of the U.S.

- European cars cut into American domestic and foreign markets.

- Western Europe became the world's largest exporter of dairy products.

- The Federal Republic of Germany had a gross national product that was exceeded only by the economies of the U.S. and the USSR.

- Western Europe and Japan were whittling away at the American economic lead in production and trade, bringing to a close the era of the dollar's unchallenged supremacy.
  - However, the dollar would remain the desired world currency for decades and into the foreseeable future

- **<u>The Communist World: The USSR and Eastern Europe</u>**

- <u>Stalinism in the Postwar Years</u>

- Died in 1953

- What he accomplished:
  - Industrialized the USSR
  - Rallied the country during WWII
  - Expanded the nation's borders
  - Developed nuclear power

- One of most costliest experiments in social engineering: Millions were dead (famines, purges), forced collectivization, loss of freedom and de-incentivization of labor
- Stalinist terror
  - Mass deportations
  - Forced movement to labor camps
  - Intellectual restrictions
- Khrushchev: The abortive effort at reform
- 1956: revealed the crimes of Stalin
- Promoted a limited "thaw" of cultural and political ideas
  - 1958 Boris Pasternak forbidden to receive the Nobel Prize for Dr. Zhivago (critical of 1917 revolution)
  - 1962 Solzhenitsyn allowed to publish One Day in the Live of Ivan Denisovich (critical of Stalin)
  - De-Stalinization
- Decentralization of economy
- Gave regions greater authority over sectors of the economy to promote efficiency and productivity (quantity over quality)
  - Soviet economy still highly centralized compared to the west; extremely sluggish
- 1958 Sputnik was launched
- Military buildup was continuing
- Problems: poverty (alcoholism, incomplete cultural development), revamping of collectivized agriculture failed
- Khrushchev's fall because of:
- Cuban missile crisis
- Openly clashed with Communist China
- Failure of agricultural policies
- Failed reform within the party
- Seen as weak by members of Politburo
- Eastern Europe: The decades of communist dictatorship
  - Soviet satellites: Baltic states, Poland, Hungary, Romania, Bulgaria, and Czechoslovakia, East Germany
- Consolidation of communist control
  - Military occupation
  - Redistribution of land was the final blow to the old landed aristocracy of Eastern Europe
  - Nationalized the economy

- o "Fascists" were excluded from public life (included anyone *accused* of fascist tendencies)

- o Church property was confiscated; state mandated atheism in national life

- o Collectivization of agriculture was resisted by peasantry and ineffective (resulted in loss of agricultural output and famine)

- o Emphasis on heavy industry and neglect of consumer goods led to low living standards

- o Much of the economic trade, benefited the USSR

- o Tito of Yugoslavia resists Soviets (but remains within the communist orbit)

- <u>Ferment and repression in East Germany, Poland, and Hungary, 1953-1956</u>
- Death of Stalin and the thaw under Khrushchev prompted challenges from the Block nations
- 1956 revolt in Poland under Gomulka

- o Reform oriented leaders loosened economic restrictions, but did not threaten the political regime)

- o Khrushchev backed down

- Revolt in Hungary under Nagy

- o Moscow sent in troops and put down the revolt (Kadar placed in power)

- o Harsh reprisals were made against the agitators

- **<u>The Communist, World: Mao Zedong and the People's Republic of China</u>**
- <u>The Civil War</u>
- 1949 war between the Chinese Communist party under Zedong and the Nationalists under Chiang Kai-shek
- US supported the Nationalist troops
- Communists steadily advanced against the Nationalist leadership

- o At first only control remote portions of the interior, Chiang controls major cities and coastline

- o Will gather strength and gradually push toward Beijing

- Nationalists were forced to leave for Taiwan (becomes the recognized "Republic of China" in the UN)
- Mao's proclamation of the "People's Republic of China"
- <u>Mao Zedong</u>
- Reflected the anti-western sentiment
- Strove to modernize China (based on Soviet model)
- Massive purges of the population were perpetrated (landlords, counterrevolutionaries, "rightists")
- Collectivization of agriculture was attempted
- 5 year plans directed toward industry

- The Great Leap Forward
    - To add decentralized means of production to the efforts of industrialization
    - To increase agricultural production (planting uncultivated land, hybridization)
    - Disaster followed (30 million died from famine) because peasants resisted collectivization (same results as seen in other places)!
- Advances under Mao Zedong
    - Eventual increase in industrial output
    - Atomic bomb developed
    - Decreased illiteracy
    - Women's rights (foot binding banned)
- Cultural Revolution
    - Mao mobilized the Red Guards (youth) against the bureaucracy and portions of the population which resisted change
    - Most prominent target was the intelligentsia
    - Used as a means to purge opponents and dissent
    - Army was eventually mobilized against the Red Guards
    - Left China in a state of confused grieving
- Mao died in 1976: considered both a modernist and hero of anti-imperialists by the left, as well as a ruthless dictator responsible for deaths of millions by historical analysts
- <u>Foreign Affairs</u>
- China maintained a lukewarm relationship with the USSR early on, begins to get colder by the mid-1960s
- Aggressive foreign policy (as evidenced in Korea)
- Claimed Tibet 1950, and conflict with India
- Relationship with USSR cooled over territorial clashes and ideological clashes (conflict over Cambodia), by 1971 relations with the US improved (to counterbalance the Soviets)
- Post-Mao China was moving toward a more peaceful relationship with its people and its neighbors
- People's Republic of China is now one of the great potential centers of global power

CHAPTER 13

THE END OF IMPERIALISM & THE START OF NEW NATIONS

- Colonial powers began to liquidate their colonial holdings
- Britain surrendered Hong Kong to China (1997); Portugal gave China Macao (1999)
- Imperialist colonial experience lefts theses regions of the world underdeveloped economically
- Became known as the "Third World" or "developing nations"

END OF THE EUROPEAN EMPIRES IN ASIA

End of the British Empire in Asia

- 1947= GB leaves India
- Indian Nat'l Congress (1885)
    - ○ Demanded independence
    - ○ Wanted to avoid social revolution
- Muslim League (1906)
    - ○ Leader: Ali Jinnah (future leader of Pakistan)
    - ○ Spoke for Muslims of India who didn't want to live under rule of Hindus
- "Quit India" campaign succeeds in 1947 when British leave
- Republic of India (Hindu) and Islamic Republic of Pakistan (Muslim)
- Ceylon and Burma also gain independence from GB
- Independence brought communal riots between Muslims and Hindus in India
    - ○ Worst violence in Punjab province
- Jawaharlal Nehru
    - ○ Indian prime minister from 1947 to 1964
    - ○ Parliamentary democracy / Fabian socialism
    - ○ 16 languages were recognized by Indian government
    - ○ Economic planning

- o Government controls on the economy; sought modern industrial and mixed economy
  - o Nationalization of key industries
  - o Condemned Chinese occupation of Tibet in 1950
  - o Retained deep antagonism toward Western imperialism and capitalism
  - o Non-aligned movement
- Rivalry with Pakistan since its inception (was once part of India under British rule)
- War over Kashmir
  - o Territorial dispute in the Himalayas
  - o 1948 fighting broke out between India and Pakistan
  - o Again in 1965, ends in uneasy truce
- 1971- war, India supported Bangladesh in seceding from Pakistan
- 1962- India vs. China regarding border disputes

Nehru's Successors

- 1966- Indira Gandhi (Nehru's daughter) becomes prime minister
  - o Strong-willed leader
  - o Pledged to eliminate poverty
  - o Made deals with Hindu nationalists
  - o 1975- proclaimed emergency rule; feared loss of power; suspended constitutional government and had opponents arrested
  - o Driven out of office
  - o Returned as Prime Minister in 1980; misguidedly sent troops to invade Golden Temple at Amritsar
  - o 1984- assassinated by Sikh soldiers
- 1984- Rajiv Gandhi (Indira's son) became prime minister
  - o Not very interested in politics
  - o Tolerant secular India came about
  - o Indian People's Party (BJP) gained popularity - Hindu revivalism
- 1991- V. Narashima Rao
  - o Leader of Congress party
  - o Reform the party
  - o Reduce bureaucracy
  - o Curb corruption
  - o Laxed economic controls, promotes growth
  - o Encourage foreign investment
  - o Reduced trade barriers
- 1992- Muslims and Hindus clash over religious sites

- 1996- Sonia Gandhi (Rajiv's widow) was chosen to lead the party
- Janata party replaced Congress party
- 1974- India tested nuclear weapons
- 1998- Pakistan tested nuclear weapons

Fifty Year of Independence

- 1997, celebrate 50 years of Indian independence
- 1997- V.R. Narayan elected president, was an untouchable
- Death rates declined
- Population triples
- However, 40% of the population was still poor
- End of century, 600 million people could vote
  - "Invisible majority"- bribery and corruption continued, the needy millions remained neglected

Islamic Republic of Pakistan

- Independence leader was Muhammad Ali Jinnah
- Succumbed to military rule
- East Pakistan proclaimed independence as Bangladesh (1971)
  - Bangladeshis supported by India
  - Pakistani government sends troops to suppress revolt
  - Civil war ensues
- 1977- military takes over Pakistan, president Ali Bhutto killed
- 1988 - Benazir Bhutto (daughter of Ali Bhutto) became first female prime minister of a major Islamic nation
  - Provoked opposition from Muslim militants
  - Forced out of office for corruption
- Became bombarded with Muslim refugees in 1979 fleeing Afghanistan
- 1999 - Army leader General Musharraf staged a military coup

The Union of Burma (Myanmar)

- Burma became independent in 1948
- Changed name to "Myanmar" in 1989
- World's largest exporter of rice
- Aung San was supposed to become 1st prime minister but was assassinated
- U Nu became first prime minister
  - Anti-imperialism, anti-capitalism, socialization
- Faced armed rebellion from insurgent separatist minorities
- 1962- head of army General Ne Win staged military take over

- National League for Democracy
  - 1980's new opposition party emerged
  - Headed by Aung San Suu Kyi
    - Went to Oxford
- 1990- military agreed to open elections
  - But when democrats won 90% of votes and 4/5ths of parliamentary seats, military proclaimed elections null and void
- Suu Kyi became a symbol of democratic aspirations; won Nobel Peace Prize in 1991

Malaysia

- 1957- gained independence from Britain
- 1962- joined Singapore to form Federation of Malaysia; Singapore withdrew in 1965
- 1969- ethnic conflicts
- Tin, rubber, oil, and lumber resources
- Ambitious construction projects
- Climbed out of Third World status!

End of the Dutch Empire: Indonesia

- Sukarno proclaimed independence in 1945; gained independence in 1949
- 4th most populous country in the world
- Modified form of Malay (official language)
- Largest Islamic population in the world
- 1959- Sukarno became populist dictator using "guided democracy"
- 1955- hosted meeting of 29 nations to rejoice in their new sovereignty and condemn Western imperialist and capitalism and pledge neutrality in Cold War
- 1965- Suharto ousts Sukarno
  - Ran the island under system of controlled elections
- Capital= Jakarta
- Economy expanded; 1997 financial panic due to foreign debt and loans
- Suharto forced out in 1998; successor H.J. Habibe
- 1999- President Wahid took office; Sukarnoputri was vice president

End of the French Colonial Empire: Indochina

- Open warfare broke out in Vietnam in 1946 b/w French and China
- Ho Chi Minh
  - Communist leader in Vietnam
  - Returned in 1941
  - Organized Viet Minh independence movement

- o Mobilized guerrilla forces to fight the Japanese
- o Proclaimed Vietnam's independence, France tries to reclaim colony (had been driven out by Japanese), turns his army on the French
- War drained French morale and resources
- French were defeated at Dien Bien Phu in 1954
- 1954- international conference at Geneva, recognizes independence of Vietnam, Cambodia and Laos
- Partitioned at 17th parallel
- US backs the South Vietnam against Ho Chi Minh, will become more involved militarily in 1960's as communist infiltration of the south intensifies

The Americans and the Philippines

- 1934- US Congress grants the Philippines self-governing commonwealth status
- 1946- independence
- 1965- Ferdinand E. Marcos became president
  - o Governed as a dictator
  - o Staunch anticommunist
- 1983- Opposition leader Benigno Aquino assassinated
- 1986- Corazon Aquino (Benigno's widow) ran against Marcos and won
  - o She restored democratic elections and civil rights
  - o Land and other reforms

THE AFRICAN REVOLUTION

- o 800 languages spoken in Africa
- o 870,000,000 Africans by 2000
- o 53 nations
- French North Africa
  - o Libya independent in 1951, Morocco & Tunisia in 1956
  - o Morocco became a constitutional monarchy
  - o Tunisia was governed by Habib Bourguiba for 30 years.
    - He introduced many democratic reforms such as women's divorce rights.
- Algeria
  - o After WWII, Algerian nationalists pressed for complete independence
  - o War broke out in 1954 and the National Liberation Front (FLN) fought against the French
    - 500,000 French troops fought Algerians. De Gaulle came to power promising to keep Algeria French, but in 1961 he supported Algerian independence.

- *Colons* in Algeria rebelled; attempted coup by French Foreign Legion; and continued fighting. Algeria became independent by 1962 nonetheless. Europeans were ejected from Algeria.
  - o The FLN governed the country for another 30 years militarily.
    - Became increasingly corrupt.
    - Mismanaged the country; became heavily dependent on oil exports.
      - Oil dependence led to widespread unemployment when oil prices dropped.
    - The FLN allowed Islamic extremists to grow in political influence:
      - The Islamic Salvation Front (anti-Western, anti-women's rights)
      - The Islamic Salvation Front gained power and won elections against the FLN. The FLN declared the party illegal and ethnic battles broke out. After 1992, Algeria was in a violent and turbulent political stage.
- End of British Rule in West Africa
  - o British government want to expedite the independence of African colonies by this time
  - o Gold Coast (Ghana) was the first British colony to gain independence
    - Civil disobedience leader Kwame Nkrumah became the prime minister.
    - The colony gained full independence in 1957
      - Nkrumah became president in 1960
      - Was anti-Western, president for life, hosted the firsts All-African People's Congress in Accra, softened ties w / the USSR and China
      - Ghana produced plentiful amounts of cocoa & gold
      - Economic decline as a result of ill-conceived projects
    - Nkrumah was ousted in 1966.
    - Military coups and political turmoil lasted until 1979 when Flight Lieutenant Jerry John Rawlings seized control, instituted a program of self-sufficiency, Rawlings offered a promise of a more liberal regime (with multi-party elections). He surrendered his power in the late 1990s.
- Nigeria
  - o 110 millions people and 250 ethnic groups by 2000.
  - o Independent by 1960; a republic by 1963.
  - o Civil War between Hausa and Ibo (Igbo) tribes, 1 million died from the violence and starvation.

- o 1979 – civilian rule; 1985 military rule, free elections restored by 1993 (YET the elections this year, won by Moshood Abiola, were nullified and Abiola was imprisoned until his death)
  - o Decrease in oil prices crippled the Nigerian economy in the 1980s.
    - Drought, high dependence on food imports, inflation & debt.
  - o In 1999, the election was allowed and General Obesanjo
- Kenya, Tanzania, Uganda
  - o Kenya:
    - European settlers owned great tracks of land and had Kenyans and Indians working on the plantations.
    - Jomo Kenyatta agitated for land reform and African representation
      - Europeans were committing violent acts of terrorism, the Kenyans responded, and the country gained independence in 1963.
      - Republic in 1964 – 55,000 Europeans left the country
      - 1 legal party (authoritarian regime)
      - in 1978 when Kenyatta died, Daniel arap Moi governed. Anti-Western, deterioration of economy, ethnic riots, no international aid before 2000 as agencies refused to provide aid until liberal reforms were taken.
  - o Tanzania
    - Zanzibar + Tanganyika (independent by 1961), became Tanzania in 1964
    - Julius Nyerere ruled from 1961 – 1985 (25 years)
      - 1 party state (yet another authoritarian regime)
      - Established Swahili and English as the official language
      - Nyerere's successors denationalized the state industries and put an end the socialist country Neyerere had created.
      - First multiparty elections in 1995
  - o Uganda
    - Independent by 1962
    - Ethnic problems.
    - 2/3 Christian
    - Milton Obote became leader and prime minister in 1963.
      - 1966 – Obote forced the Bugandan King to flee to the countryside. He created a powerful autocracy
      - 1971 a ruthless soldier Idi Amin rose through the ranks to become a commanding general of Uganda. He seized power. Killed 300,000 people, expelled 60,000 Asians, targeted ethnic groups

- o 1976 he declared himself "president for life"
- o 1979 over a border dispute with Tanzania, Amin was overthrown by the Tanzanian army along with Ugandan exiles
  - ▪ Obote returned to power. He was also ruthless, killing tens of thousands
    - He was overthrown by the same army that overthrew Amin by Yoweri Museveni (1986)
- Zimbabwe
  - o Formerly Southern Rhodesia
  - o Resisted British rule since 1965 for 15 years. Independent by 1980
  - o 1 party state led by Robert Mugabe who led the country for 20 years
- South Africa
  - o 30 M blacks, 6 M whites, 3 M mixed 1 M Asians.
  - o Rich in natural resources, especially gold, diamond, and strategic minerals
  - o Apartheid was established in 1948 by Afrikaners
    - ▪ Established "autonomous" tribal homelands, which in reality were dependent on white government
    - ▪ Blacks not allowed to travel outside of the homeland without passport
  - o Became the Republic of South Africa in 1961
  - o By the late 60's and 70's, apartheid protestors were global.
    - ▪ Apartheid was repealed in 1991
  - o 1994 Nelson Mandela, 1996 the country adopted a constitution and a broad bill of rights
  - o Thabo Mbeki replaced Mandela in 1999
- French Sub Saharan Africa
  - o France gave the African colonies representation in the French National Assembly in the 50's (but still controlled them)
  - o France's 15 colonies all chose independence
    - ▪ Still maintained close ties to France
  - o France still intervened heavily after 1960, examples:
    - ▪ Central African Republic. France removed a dictator but stayed there 13 years after he was removed
    - ▪ 1999 ivory coast coup
- Belgian Congo
  - o Capital: Brazzaville
  - o Ethnic groups at odds

- o Leftist leader Patrice Lumumba was assassinated in 1961
- o USSR claimed the Europeans created chaos so that the Europeans would be "forced" to return (and reinstate control like in colonial times).
- o In 1965, Colonel Joseph Désiré Mobutu established a 32 year dictatorship
  - ▪ Nationalized industries, Africanized names of places & things; the country became Zaire. He changed his name to Mobutu Sese Seko.
  - ▪ Leopoldville renamed Kinshasa; Stanleyville renamed Kisangani
- o Became the Democratic republic of Congo in 1997
- o Laurent Kabila took over. He was assassinated in 2001; 5 countries were at war in DRC
- Rwanda & Burundi
  - o Rwanda
    - ▪ Hutu & Tutsti (Watutsi) ethnic groups
      - • After WWII Tutsti were favored by imperialists over Hutus; seen as more industrious and better facial features
    - ▪ Hutu saw independence as an opportunity to get revenge on the Tutsi
    - ▪ 1994: Massacre of the Tutsti by Hutu; 500,000 dead in weeks
  - o Burundi
    - ▪ Declared a republic in 1966, Hutu King killed by Tutsti
    - ▪ 1993 presidential elections in Rwanda and Burundi; April 1994 a plane carrying both presidents was shot down. WAR.
- End of the Portuguese Colonial Empire
  - o Portugal clung the longest to its colonies
  - o Had been suppressing revolts from 1961-1974
    - ▪ Angola, Mozambique and other small colonies (eg. Saõ Tome e Principe) were granted independence in 1974.
    - ▪ Communist attempted foothold in Angola
      - • Fidel Castro acts as proxy for USSR, sent 50k men to ensure the establishment of a communist government in the country. Receives aid from Soviet block.
      - • US and west supports anticommunist UNITA guerillas
      - • The outside powers withdrew in the early 1990s.
      - • Hundreds of thousands Angolans were killed
    - ▪ Communist expansion into Mozambique as well (1974 – 1990) by Cuban proxies. Establishes pro-Soviet regime. War drought and famine killed over 500,000 people.

- - Desperately turned to the West in the 1990s for economic assistance.
- Ethiopia, Eritrea, and Somalia were located on the Horn of Africa.
- They were a part of the Italian empire, but that was short lived
- Ethiopia was the last European annexation in Africa
  - Haile Selassie returned as emperor after the Italians left
  - Soviets controlled Ethiopia, then lost interest in supporting its regime
  - Eritrea was annexed by Ethiopia
- Somalia, under the Italian control before 1914, became independence in 1960
- 1977 Somalia invaded Ethiopia
- Ethiopia had Soviet military aid, which facilitated an Ethiopian victory
- 1956 Sudan received their independence
- Liberia- 1847
- Sierra Leone- capital Freetown
- "A matter defending humanity itself" - Kofi Annan
- Uhuru= freedom
- Leopold Senghor poet president of Senegal (negritude-)
- Nobel prize- Wole Soyinka 1986 1/2 of 600 mill in Africa 1$/day
- Liberia, Somalia, Zaire, Angola (4 largest African recipients of US aid)
- Musevini- no party democracy-Movement
- Turkey: Kemal Ataturk
- Muhammad, Allah Mecca to Medina, caliph
- Near east- bordering the Mediterranean (Asia Minor)
- Middle east- midway between Europe and E. Asia
  - Now the Middle East - Predominately Islamic religion
  - Non Arab- Indonesia, Malaysia, Pakistan, Bangladesh, Afghanistan, Iran
  - Koran or Qur'an
    - Egypt- 1922
    - Iraq- 1932-1945
    - League of Arab States: 1945 (Egypt Iraq Lebanon Saudi Arabia Syria Jordan
    - Libya- 1951
    - PLO- Palestine Liberation Organization
- Zionism- established a Jewish homeland in Palestine
  - Small number of Jews from Russia and Eastern Europe emigrated to Palestine before 1914
  - Balfour Declaration- 1917 "Jewish homeland in Palestine"

- Israeli Conflicts
  - 1947- UN adopted recommendation of partitioning Palestine (part Jewish, part Arab, and with area around Jerusalem under international control)
  - May 1948- Syria, Lebanon, Jordan, Egypt, Iraq refused recognition and invaded Israel
  - Armistice of 1949- Jerusalem came under divided control, amount Israeli allotted land increased by ½
  - Democratically elected parliament in Israel- the Knesset
  - Kibbutzim: labor unions and agricultural cooperatives
  - Israel (with France and British allies) went to war with Egypt in 1956 to seize control of Suez Canal (they attempted to bar Israeli shipping)
  - 967- Israel waged the Six Day War vs. Egypt, Syria, Jordan (Egypt moved to close to Gulf of Aqaba to Israel
  - 1973- Egyptian and Syrian forces attacked Israelis on Yom Kippur (when Israelis were close to victory, League of Arab States introduced an embargo on oil shipments-quadrupled the price of oil).
  - 1982- Israel invaded Lebanon
  - 1964- Under Yasir Arafat the PLO became a full member of the Arab League
  - 1971- Labor for the first time lost control of the government to a conservative: Likud Party with Menachem Begin as Prime Minister
  - 1980- unified the Israeli capital by annexing East Jerusalem
  - 1987- nationalist agitation by young Palestinians-- intifada
  - 1992- Labor coalition returned to office headed by Yitzhak Rabin and Shimon Peres
  - Oslo Accords: Israel recognized the PLO as the representative of the Palestinian people and agreed to initial steps for Palestine self-government
  - 1995- Killed P.M. Yitzhak Rabin, by a Jewish extremist who was opposed to Rabin's signing of the Oslo Accord
  - Benjamin Netanyahu- new Likud leader
  - Ehud Barak- military man and former Israeli chief of staff (representing Labor) He withdrew Israeli armed forces from its southern Lebanon security zone
  - New intifada broke out when Ariel Sharon, former army commander, became Prime Minister in early 2001
- Libya
  - Oil in Libya (1959)
  - 1969- Colonel Muhammad al-Qaddafi established a dictatorship. Libya became headquarters for terrorism and Soviet proxy
- Syria: Hafez al-Assad rises to power and remains leader for 30 years
- Iran- Persian language, Shiite state, allied with US and west under Shah
  - Persia (became Iran in 1935)- 1921 Reza Khan assumed title as Shah and

1925 embarked on a program of modernization

- Prime Minister of Persia- Mossadegh (leftist), overthrown by US orchestrated coup

- Ayatollah Ruhollah Khomeini- returned from exile in Paris ("Islamic Republic")

    o Women ordered to wear the chador (traditional long black dress)

    o Necktie outlawed for men, encouraged to grow beards

    o Authorities banned western music, radio, TV, and enforced Islamic prohibition on alcohol

    o "The Great Satan"- Ayatollah Khomeini's description of the US

- 1980 war broke out when Iraq launched an attack on Iranian territory. (Iraq-Saddam Hussein) Land war became a tanker war in the Persian Gulf involving Saudi Arabia, Kuwait and others

    o By 1987- Iranian counteroffensive failed

    o August 1988- Iran accepted a cease-fire

    o 8 year war

- 1980 President Muhammed Khatami- platform of political, economic reform, civil society, rule of law, freer atmosphere

Iraq and the Persian Gulf War of 1990-1991

- Iraq emerged from war with Iran with troubled economy. Saddam Hussein was determined to reverse his country's fortunes!

- Aug 1990 – invaded and annexed oil rich Kuwait (expanding influence in region and threatening Saudi Arabia)

- Multinational Western and Arab military coalition build up in Saudi Arabia (Saudi's were major oil exporters to western nations)

- Operation Desert Storm: 1991 – air attack and ground assault, forcing Iraq to withdraw from Kuwait

- No effort made to remove Hussein from power after liberating Kuwait; fears that it would create a power vacuum in Middle East and more instability

- Iraq continues to challenge UN ban on manufacture of weapons of mass destruction

Changes in the Middle East

- Islamic world caught between traditional religious and social beliefs and modern economic and cultural changes

- Religious radicalism (starting with the Iranian Revolution of 1979)

    o Rejected secularism, sought Islamic theocracies

    o Women segregated and deprived of educational/vocational opportunities to "protect them from dangers of modern world"

    o Taliban movement: took control of Afghanistan in 1990s, after war with USSR

        ➢ Strictest forms of repression (women stay at home, dress codes)

> ➢ Punishment according to sharia law (centuries-old Islamic legal code)

- o Egypt: government outlawed Muslim Brotherhood, but Islamic leaders rally youth in Cairo protesting sponsorship of books they consider blasphemous to Islam

- o Turkey: army protects secular tradition

- o Algeria: after military government rejection of election results in 1991 (Islamic party won), armed groups conducted massacres

- o Sudan: Islamic regime in north, military campaign to enforce Islam on entire country

- Increased sentiment for more flexible interpretation of Koranic law

  - o Saudi Arabia: women can't drive or be in public unaccompanied by male family member; amputation and beheading as punishment – people urge modification of these practices

  - o Egypt: 2000 – women free to divorce husband without their consent (one of most far-reaching reforms of family law)

  - o Kuwait: emir declares women can vote and compete in elections – this is initially blocked, but soon put into practice

- Region is still highly authoritarian – lacked independent political parties and credible parliaments, outcomes of elections are predictable

- Access to outside world made a difference – globalization!

CHANGING LATIN AMERICA

- 1945 – most nations had already been independent for over a century, but many problems could be traced to colonial period!

- 7 million square miles – includes Mexico, Central America, South America, Caribbean Islands

- Spanish, Portuguese (Brazil), English and French (Caribbean)

- Racially diverse (whites and mestizos tend to dominate)

- Of 10 most populous cities, 4 are in Latin America: Mexico City, Sao Paulo, Rio de Janeiro, Buenos Aires

The Colonial Experience and the Wars for Independence

- Spanish incorporated Indians into colonial system and imposed social hierarchy

- Crown granted large estates to Spanish nobles to encourage settlement: encomiendas

- Roman Catholic missionaries help settle and bring European culture

- Indians repressed: worked on estates, and underground silver mines

- Arrival of Europeans resulted demographic disaster (disease, superior armaments and technology)

- Imported black slaves from Africa to work on sugar plantations

- Slavery essentially abolished by 1850s, but forms of servitude (peonage) still remained, Indians and blacks are still lowest on social hierarchy

- Wealth of colonies exported to "mother" country, finished goods imported into colonies (mercantilism)

- Ranching and mining became large scale, new commercial enterprises arose (disliked by nobles and creoles – American-born Spanish)

- Church owned ½ of productive land by 1800

- Creoles gain power, and from 1808-1826, fight for independence (when Napoleon occupies Spain and Portugal)

  o Frightened by violence of French Revolution want to keep their power

  o Status of lower classes unimproved

  o Military class and caudillos (dictators) emerge

- Dependency on outside world led to Britain (Industrial Revolution) establishing strong ties to Latin American markets – this economic penetration by Britain (and soon US) called neocolonialism: economic domination that did not require acquisition of territory.

- Outside investments and European immigration into Latin America strengthens economy

The Colossus to the North

- Europeans might have gained economic control of unstable governments, however:

- Monroe Doctrine: opposed continental interference with independence of new states

- Roosevelt Corollary 1904: US alone would assume responsibility of intervention for purposes of restoring stability, protecting investments, collecting debts

- US policy of "dollar diplomacy" (active armed intervention) especially in Central America and Caribbean until mid-1930s

- Early 20th century: US rivals Britain as dominant trading partner of Latin America; after WWI, replaces Britain as source of loans and capital investment

- Latin America remains undeveloped due to dependency on outside world, and impoverished masses provide weak consumer base

Economic Growth and its Problems

- Latin America suffers from Great Depression: fall of prices and evaporation of foreign investment

- This (and WWII) encourages them to industrialize (ex: Brazil under Getulio Vargas 1930-45)

- Economic structure changes significantly after 1945 (benefited from increased demand for raw materials and influx of foreign investment)

- Alliance for Progress (sponsored by US in early 1960s under Kennedy) – new North American commitment to development of LA

- Economies grew steadily from 1945-75

- New industrialized countries: Mexico, Argentina, Brazil, Chile

- Industrialization still occurred under protective tariffs, subsidies, and state-controlled enterprises, low mass-purchasing power

  o Economic expansion mostly benefited social elites

- 1970s: become heavily in debt; by 1980, this is a serious financial threat – ease interest payments.
  - Reduced the already depressed living standards
  - Inflation rates of over 1000%
  - Agricultural prices collapse, economic growth slowed (1%) or was even negative
  - 1980s a "lost decade"
- Real growth gradually resumed: abandoned state controls, encouraged freer market economies, sounder public finances, brought inflation under control
- Population growth was a concern!
  - Church's prohibition of birth control
  - Population tripled between 1950 and 1990s
  - Diminished social and economic gains because of this
  - Population stabilized in more industrialized countries
- Rural workers go to cities
- Upper-class minority monopolizes wealth and land (40% live in poverty)
- Haiti and Honduras some of poorest nations in world; Bolivia had lowest per capita income
- 1960s: "liberation theology"/"church of the poor"
- Mexico: revolution of 1910 – church and military power is curbed, land redistribution
  - Institutional Revolutionary Party (PRI) now only revolutionary in name – dominant political organization
  - Promoted modernization, but there was widespread nepotism and corruption, social neglect
  - 1994 revolt of Indian-led peasant movement in Chiapas
  - Citizens are distrustful of politicians
  - 2000 – PRI defeated by centrist Vincente Fox

End of Yankee Imperialism?
- "Good neighbor" policy of US in 1930s – steps away from interventionist policy
- Resentment in Latin America due to interventions before 1933 in Mexico, Nicaragua, Panama, DR, Haiti
- Post WWII interventions tied to Cold War and containment: Guatemala (1954), Dominican Republic (1965-66), Grenada (1983), Panama (1989)
- 1948: Organization of American States (OAS) – 35 nations in Western hemisphere join together to settle disputes
- US agrees to hand over Panama canal in 1977, occurs in 1999
- Growing sense of economic interdependence
  - US needed a prospering Latin America for its own economy

- o 1994: North American Free Trade Agreement between US, Canada, Mexico: eventually will eliminate all trade barriers between these 3 countries
- o Increased immigration to US

<u>The Political Record</u>

- Insecure constitutional regimes, repressive military dictatorships, civil wars and social revolution, ethnic tensions and labor unrest, agitation against foreign (US) interests

- Some populist governments with mass political support
  - o Brazil – Vargas 1930-45, 1951-54
  - o Argentina – Juan Perón 1946-55

- Central America: political instability and anti-Communist sentiments result in US support for rightist elements, example: Nicaragua and El Salvador

- Leftist regimes overthrown, often with unofficial US help, harsh repression followed and political opponents "disappeared"
  - o Argentina's "Dirty War" against leftists 1976-83
  - o Chile: Left coalition under Allende elected in 1970 (land reform, nationalization of coal mines) toppled 3 years later by military with US help (House of Spirits!)
    - ➤ Marxist president Salvador Allende is killed
    - ➤ New regime headed by General Augusto Pinochet
    - ➤ Pinochet establishes repressive dictatorship; there was economic growth, but country is still divided politically

- Radical social changes came from Cuba
  - o 1933: "revolt of the sergeants" led by Fulgencio Batista overthrows dictator Gerardo Machado; becomes head of armed forces, and exercises great influence in Cuban politics
  - o Serves as democratically elected president from 1940-44
  - o Runs for president in 1952, and facing defeat at the polls orchestrates a coup. Will rule until 1959: Fidel Castro and leftist guerrillas overthrow him; promise land reform and economic dependence on US
  - o US trade embargo due to Castro confiscating American corporate investments and landholdings
  - o On April 17, 1961, 1400 CIA trained Cuban exiles launched failed invasion at the Bay of Pigs on the south coast of Cuba
  - o Castro moves closer to Soviets (Cuban Missile Crisis – brink of nuclear war!)
  - o Cuba: only professedly Marxist country in Western hemisphere
  - o Castro champions anti-imperialism, aids leftist movements in Bolivia and Central America, supports anti-colonial guerrilla armies in Africa

- o Cuba becomes Soviet clone state: expands network of social services, public health, literacy, improved life for rural masses – but economic failures and totalitarianism coercion

  - o Increasing dependent on Soviets for economic aid (exports sugar, imports oil)

  - o Castro was first secretary of the Cuban Communist Party (only one allowed) and ruled as dictator

  - o Political opponents executed or imprisoned, many flee the island

  - o Castro becomes isolated figure internationally with collapse of USSR 1989-91; decline of *Fidelismo*

- Beginning of 21st C: many Latin American countries moving toward stable constitutional governments, softening ideological conflicts, loosening state controls over economy

- Still important issues: inflation, heavy debt, currency crises, population growth (impedes socioeconomic growth of lower classes)

- Constitutional democracies were fragile: military continues to seek power, increased crime rates, still poverty and social inequities

- Venezuela had been leader in civilian democratic rule since 1958

  - o In spite of oil wealth, still was poverty and inequity

  - o Hugo Chavez elected 1998 – called for "peaceful social revolution"

  - o Wrote a new constitution, reelected in 2000 (will become a leftist dictator)

- In late 1990s Latin America moving toward privatization, free trade, open markets, globalization

- A new generation of young leftist activists was arising – attacked global economy (claims that only benefits wealthy

- Many financial crises and flight of capital from leftist policies

- By 2008 left-leaning leaders of Bolivia, Brazil and Chile meet at the Union of South American Nations summit

THE DEVELOPING WORLD

The Experience of Development

- After WWII, US takes greater role in assisting countries (part of containment strategy)

- It was believed that developing nations were on their way to modernization, economic growth, and social progress. However, not all leaders in developing countries will follow free market model

  - o Some leaders believed central planning, nationalized economies, and government controls would accomplish this faster

  - o Nehru in India and others follow heavily socialized capitalist state with 5 year plans (inspired by, but not duplicating USSR/Chinese model), others follow Japanese model of private capitalism in partnership with government

- International agencies helped finance projects for agriculture, industry, health, education

- 1960s: "development decade"

- o Kennedy wanted to raise "banner of hope" for the poor
- o Industrialization could end excessive dependence on imports
- o "Green Revolution" of agriculture in US increased productivity
- Advances didn't bring much change in global economic position (still didn't share in economic expansion, gap between rich and poor widening)
- Late 1960s – developing nations ask for "new international economic order" to increase access to funds, markets, technology, and shirt international financing to broader control
- Third World Bloc of neutralist, nonaligned states (25, beginning in 1961) – increasingly critical of wealthier west
- Extensive debt (especially in oil-producing countries) due to decline in trade and world prices. 1/3 debt was from Argentina, Brazil, Mexico, Venezuela
- Agricultural production couldn't keep up with population growth
- To finance industrialization, governments encourage export of crops and neglect production of food for their own population (agricultural economy considered inferior)
- Many of the new industrial products failed to compete internationally and within each country!
- Rush for development, clumsy bureaucracies, extravagant spending, corruption
  - Rural populations are still very poor
  - People move to cities, only to suffer from joblessness, overcrowding, and pollution

Changing World and Persistent Problems

- 1 billion people impoverished by 2000
- Some countries leaving "Third World" status and forming intermediate category of "newly industrialized countries"
- "Least-developed countries" including many in Sub-Saharan Africa, Bangladesh, Haiti: a "Fourth World"
- Countries that developed most rapidly had market economies.
  - Debate concerning reliance on the market: "maldistribution" of wealth
  - Only two worlds (rich and poor) by 2000!

Reappraising Development

- World Bank and IMF shift from "growth and development" to "poverty reduction"
- World Bank had previously only judged success quantitatively
  - Now, foreign aid must go not only to central governments, but also local ones
  - Human development indexes now not only focus on per capita income, but also literacy, life expectancy, health, nutrition, status of women and children
  - Donor countries agreed to cancel debts of poorest countries
- IMF was heavily criticized for reorienting economic development in countries without consideration of social or political consequences

- Impact of global economic integration
  - Critics: increased poverty, increased social divides, hurt environment, exploited local population, used child labor, international corporations from developed countries have the greatest control
  - Pros: free trade and IT stimulates economy and will eventually help poor

Dr. Juan R. Céspedes, Ph.D.

CHAPTER 14

CONFRONTATION & COEXISTENCE

Late 1950s:

- o Western Europe and Japanese economies rebuilt (with massive American aid)
- o Former European colonies asserting independence
- o China becomes a major Communist power
- o Escalating nuclear arms race
- o 'Bipolarity' (predominance of two super powers - US and Soviet Union) gave way to new global configurations

- Confrontation and Détente, 1955-1975
  - o Soviet leaders after Stalin more conciliatory
  - o *Periods of détente* (formal relaxation of tensions)
  - o 1955:
    - Cold War stabilized
    - Korean War over, focus on containment in Asia
    - NATO faced Warsaw Pact nations
    - Western Powers and Soviet Union agree on treaty with Austria ending joint Allied occupation = Austria is independent and neutral
    - US/Eisenhower, Britain, France, meet at Geneva with Soviet leaders
      - Friendlier atmosphere than previously under Stalin
      - No new agreements but 'spirit of conciliation and cooperation'
  - o Khrushchev: dominant Soviet Leader
    - Rejected inevitability of war
    - Emphasized 'possibility and necessity of *peaceful coexistence'*
  - o Eisenhower ("53-"61) continued containment, buildup of military
  - o Sec. of State Dulles urges 'rollback' of Soviet power

- Soviets angry that East Germans are fleeing to West Berlin and Federal Republic of Germany
    - Demand western powers to leave West Berlin
    - Eisenhower says no!
- 1959: Khrushchev visits Eisenhower at Camp David, talk about the need for peaceful coexistence and disarmament
- Cooperation fades when Khrushchev subjected to pressure from the Kremlin and Mao saying he's too friendly with the West
    - Khrushchev produces evidence of American reconnaissance flights over Soviet territory
    - By summer of 1960 'spirit of Geneva/Camp David' gone
- Americans protested but did not intervene when the Soviets:
    - 1953: put down anticommunist uprising in East Berlin
    - 1956: exerted pressure on Poland to curb reform movement
    - 1956: sent troops/tanks to put down Hungarian revolt
    - 1968: crushed Czech uprising
- 1956: Suez Crisis
    - President of Egypt Gamal Abdel Nasser's decides 26 July 1956 to nationalize the Suez Canal
    - Britain, France, & Israel attack Egypt to regain Western control of the canal and to remove Nasser from power.
    - They are successful in attaining their military objectives, but pressure from the United States, the USSR, and the United Nations ...
    - Convinces Britain, France, and Israel to withdraw (might push other Middle Eastern countries into Soviet sphere of influence)
- *American Cold War Policy* mainly consisted of the Eisenhower Doctrine, which pledged protection to any government fighting international communism
    - Dispatches troops to Lebanon 1958
    - Operation Blue Bat: intended to bolster the pro-Western Lebanese government of President Camille Chamoun against internal opposition and threats from Syria and Egypt.
    - The operation involved approximately 14,000 men, and successfully intimidated Camille's opposition
    - US withdrew its forces on October 25, 1958.
- October 1957: Soviets launch Sputnik
    - US worried, intensifies research and launches Explorer I a few months later
- 1958: Soviets develop intercontinental ballistic missiles (ICBM)

- So the US makes ICBMs, and the arms race takes on a different and more menacing dimension
- *New kind of arms race* develops based on 'mutual deterrence'
  - 1966: De Gaulle removes France from NATO military command
- **The Kennedy Years, 1961-1963**
  - Increased foreign aid, sponsored Peace Corps
  - *Kennedy intervenes in Cuba:*
    - Some in JFK's administration thought Castro was disposed to democracy: he wasn't
    - Castro institutes agrarian reforms, imprisoned/executed political prisoners
    - Soon joined ranks with the Cuban Communist Party
    - Eisenhower had imposed a strict embargo due to Cuban expropriation of American businesses
    - Castro gets closer to Soviet Union
    - CIA secretly trains Cuban refugees for armed invasion
      - *Bay of Pigs:*
        - Kennedy inherited the plans for the invasion from Eisenhower
        - April 1961: Invasion lacks air support, fails, most of the 1500 invaders captured
        - Castro openly Marxist-Leninist
        - US tightens embargo
  - Meeting with Kennedy in Vienna, Soviets demand US leaves Berlin again, the US rejects demands
  - 1961: Soviets construct *Berlin Wall,* hundreds trying to cross were killed
- The Cuban Missile Crisis of 1962:
  - Soviets plan to construct missile sites in Cuba
  - Kennedy blockades Cuba, prepares US planes and airborne troops for invasion
  - Khrushchev backs down, removes missile sites in return for US pledge not to invade Cuba, remove US missiles in Turkey and Northern Italy
  - Cuba agreement: USSR given a base from which to spread communism in the Americas
  - 1964: Khrushchev seen as weak by Kremlin Politburo and ousted, replaced by Brezhnev
- The United States and the Vietnam War
  - The containment policy entangled the United States in the Vietnam War.
    - Communist leader Ho Chi Minh led an anti-colonial war against

146

French for over 8 years ('46-'54). The French eventually acknowledged defeat, recognizing the independence of Vietnam, Laos, and Cambodia in 1954.

- Vietnam was divided into the communist north and the anticommunist, south.

○ Northern Vietnam was led by Ho Chi Minh and the capital Hanoi.

- South Vietnam was backed by Western countries and lead by Ngo Dinh Diem.

- South Vietnam's capital was Saigon.

○ Vietnam was partitioned at 17th parallel until general elections could be held in 1956, but South Vietnam refused to take part in countrywide elections, fearing fraud by communists.

- The Viet Cong, supplied by the North, undermined the South Vietnamese government by waging a guerrilla war in the countryside.

- At this time, the National Liberation Front (the political arm of the Viet Cong) emerges as rival civil authority, and encouraged the participation of non-communists in the insurgency (although they will be under communist control).

○ Ho Chi Minh was supported financially and militarily by the Soviet Union and The Peoples Republic of China. To prevent other Southeast Asian countries from succumbing to communism i.e., the "Domino Theory"), the US sends aid and advisors to South Vietnam.

○ American economic support of anticommunists in South Vietnam spans five presidencies: from Eisenhower in the 1950s to Ford in 1974.

○ In 1964, American air strikes were ordered after the North Vietnamese allegedly attacked US destroyers in Gulf of Tonkin.

- Gulf of Tonkin Resolution gave President Johnson authorization, without a formal declaration of war by Congress, for the use of "*conventional*" military force in Southeast Asia.

- He was now authorized to to assist militarily any member or protocol state of the Southeast Asia Collective Defense Treaty.

○ 1965: US Marines arrive to root out Viet Cong; US conducts 'search and destroy' missions, burns villages suspected of collaborating with communists and resettles population into secure areas.

- In 1966 there were 200,000 troops; in 1969: 550,000 there were troops

○ Unable to overcome North Vietnamese persistence; Tet offensive shook US complacency about outcome of war.

- Tet a military defeat for communists, but to the American public made the US look like it was fighting an unsuccessful war.

○ Negotiations seemed necessary, There was criticism of US involvement by allies in Western Europe.

- Protests were prevalent on college campuses and cities, especially due to conscription (the "draft").

o Johnson was focused with winning.

- He was convinced it was in US' interest to contain communism in Southeast Asia.

- The war resulted in Johnson not running again for re-election in 1968.

- Presidential candidate Richard Nixon pledges early end to war and 'Vietnamization'.

- Once in office, he shifts responsibility to South Vietnam, started gradual withdrawal of American troops, and restarted stalemated peace talks.

o Nixon and Kissinger (US national security advisor) continue the war heavy air attacks and bring the war into Cambodia and Laos (used by communists as a sanctuary and means to transport arms and troops into the South).

- Demonstrations mount in US against the war, cease-fire agreement in 1973.

o U.S. Withdrawal begins in 1973. Hostilities don't end and war resumes between north and south.

- Congress ordered an end to direct US military involvement in August 1973.

- US financial aid to South Vietnam was cut off by a Democratically controlled Congress in August 1974

- 1974: North Vietnam captures key cities.

- Saigon fell to the communists in April 1975.

  • Saigon renamed Ho Chi Minh City in honor of recently passed leader (who died in 1969)

o After 30 years of fighting, there was finally peace and with it a communist victory.

- New regime launches 'political reeducation', nationalized property, moved people from cities to countryside: established communist dictatorship

- Cambodia and Laos also fall under communist control.

o Costs of the War

- 1.3. million Vietnamese died, US had 58,000 deaths, Huge military expenditure, Caused mistrust of presidential power in US.

- At least 165,000 people died in the Socialist Republic of Vietnam's "reeducation" camps. Thousands were tortured or abused. Prisoners were incarcerated for as long as 17 years, with most terms ranging from three to 10 years.

- Hundreds of thousands flee from the communists ("boat people")
- 1973: Congress adopted legislation to curb presidential initiatives to wage war.
- There was a heavy American Moral cost: the revelation of atrocities committed by American troops (for example My Lai in 1968).
- Veterans were not respected by antiwar activists.

  o The Khmer Rouge
  - Cambodia, overthrew their government.
  - Cambodian Leader Pol Pot was a ruthless communist dictator.
  - Genocide of over two million between 1975 and 1978 in the "killing fields".
  - Wanted to create the perfect agrarian communist society
  - Pro-Chinese in regional Vietnam/China geopolitical disputes.
  - Vietnam invades Cambodia in 1979 overthrows the Khmer Rouge.
  - Soviets encourage Vietnam to leave Cambodia in the late 80s.

- Brezhnev: The 'Prague Spring'
  o Brezhnev was the dominant leader after Khrushchev.
  - Intent on building military and navy regardless of cost to compete with US.
  - 1968: democratic reforms by Alexander Dubcek threaten one party state in Czechoslovakia
  o Brezhnev crushes 'Prague spring'
  - 'Brezhnev Doctrine' mirrors Truman Doctrine, proclaims Soviet right to intervene in the name of 'proletarian internationalism' on behalf of any Communist government to prevent capitalist take-over
  - Czechoslovakia returns to communist dictatorship
  - The invasion undermined Soviet leadership of Western Communist Parties who were strongly against the brutal intervention

- Brezhnev and Nixon
  o Nixon and détente
  - Nixon intensified the war in Vietnam but sought détente
    - Nixon-Kissinger policy linked Western technology/trade/investment to Soviet cooperation in international affairs
  - Khrushchev's claim of passing the West economically was false.
    - The two Germanys recognize each other diplomatically
    - Unlike in 1945 when there were two only superpowers,

there now emerged others

- o The realization of a new superpower: The People's Republic of China
    - 1972: Nixon visits Mao, initiates diplomatic/economic relations
    - American opening to China pressures Soviets to pursue détente
- o Strategic Arms Limitations (SALT) talks resume
    - Both sign, reaffirm goal of 'peaceful coexistence'
    - Agree to reduce antimissile defense system
    - Promised continued negotiations
- o 1975: meeting at Helsinki, over two years Conference on Security and Cooperation in Europe
    - Helsinki Accords not formal treaty but ratified European territorial boundaries from post-WWII, set up committees to watch for human rights
    - However, in 1979 Soviet-Western relations take another downward turn

- The Recession: Stagnation and Inflation
    - o Different from other declines because recession is accompanied with inflation, resulting in "stagflation"
    - o 1970s: recession was world wide
    - o Over 10% of American and West Europeans labor force unemployed
        - Unemployment was considered by the left *the bane of industrial capitalism*
    - o Welfare benefits more advanced than 1930s
        - Severance pay, trade unions, etc.
    - o *Structural unemployment*: people lost jobs due to automation
    - o Western industrial countries looked to Federal Republic of Germany
        - Germany remembers the inflation of the 1920s and makes fighting that its number one priority, other countries follow suit
    - o *Faith in Keynes shaken,* his tenets challenged as never before
        - Prime Minister Margaret Thatcher and President Reagan believe the welfare state is costly and wasteful
        - Offer incentives to stimulate production rather than demand = *Supply Side economics*
            - Benefits would 'trickle down'
            - Corporate growth
            - Based on creation of capital, instead of deficit spending
    - o Return to prosperity increased faith in free-market economy
    - o 'Middle way' = market economy for growth but also limited government intervention in social and economic problems

- <u>Economic and Political Change in Western Europe</u>
  - Britain hit particularly hard by 1970 recession
    - Highest rate of inflation in industrialized countries
    - Depended on foreign loans
    - Disruptive strikes in coal and transportation weakened the country
  - Margaret Thatcher—first woman Prime Minister in any major Western country—headed Conservative government
    - Cut government expenditures
    - Reduced imports
    - Resisted trade union wage demands
    - Inflation curbed but unemployment rose
    - 1982: patriotism stirred as she sends Armada to prevent Argentina from taking Falkland/Malvina Islands
    - Returned 1/3 nationalized/government owned industries to private enterprise
    - Credit more easily available
    - Highest economic growth of any European country
    - UK again a leading creditor nation
    - Fiscal measures led to her fall in 1990
  - John Major is her successor
    - Labour party abandons idea of class struggle
    - Challenges conservatives
  - '*New Labour*' under Tony Blair
    - More moderate
  - Politics in France veered left sooner
    - 1981 moderate Socialist Francois Mitterand
    - Revitalizes Socialist Party
    - Drops class-struggle rhetoric
    - '*Changer la vie*' = Change life for everyone (his campaign slogan implying an improved life)
    - Wins presidency
      - Labor reforms introduced
      - Nationalized banks
      - Faithful to Keynesian precepts
      - Reduced French competitiveness abroad, slowed economic growth

- Leftist policies result in a sluggish economy, so he shifts policies abruptly: emphasizes modernization, government supports to technology
    - Isolated the communists, France was split and seesawed back and forth resulting in *cohabitation* = when a popularly elected president of one party governs with a prime minister who represent the opposing parliamentary majority
    - 1988: Mitterand reelected president and has his own party in National Assembly
    - Cohabitation resumes with Prime Minister Jacques Chirac
        - French economy strengthened in 1990s but unemployment still high
    - Women played a larger role in government
        - New law said women were to be candidates in equal numbers as men
        - Women admitted to previously all men French Academy
  - Socialists championed moderation and pragmatism
    - Example: Helmut Schmidt, Social Democratic Chancellor in West Germany; Bettino Craxi in Italy; Felipe Gonzalez in Spain; moderate Socialist and Social Democratic Party platforms in Portugal
  - West Germany: Schmidt looks to control inflation, resulting in policies that lead to unemployment and industrial slowdown
  - Extremist groups exploit anti-foreign sentiment, especially from Turkish immigrants
  - German Federal Republic remains most productive nation in western Europe
  - Plans for reunification of Germany still remote
    - *'One nation and two states'*
        - Willy Brandt
        - Ospolitik attempts to reconcile the two Germany's and increase trade between them
- The American Economy
  - Recovers from post-1974 recessions sooner than the Europeans
  - Deregulation of industry and corporate streamlining stimulates economic growth
  - Federal Reserve Board protects against inflation
  - Stock market began to rise
  - Setbacks:
    - Temporary fall in stock prices in 1987

- General economic slowdown after 1989
- Campaigning on sluggish economy, Clinton defeats Bush in 1992
  - ○ *Economic concerns* remained in 1980s
    - Oil crisis of 1970s reinforced demand for the dollar
    - Strong dollar = more difficult for US to sell products abroad
    - Decrease in value of the dollar resulted in increasing foreign investments in US and exports
  - ○ Japanese Economy improved enormously
    - Nomura Securities Corporation of Tokyo becomes largest Brokerage firm
  - ○ *Relative decline in growth in US* due to:
    - Inadequate American savings and investment
    - Slowdown in productivity gains
    - However US recovers faster than other countries from short-lived recession of 1990
- The Financial World
  - ○ Worlds largest stock exchanges centered in New York City
  - ○ Deregulation led to increase in acquisitions and mergers
  - ○ *Speculation and investment* blurred
  - ○ 1987 stock exchange loses ¼ of value, causes panic, but recovers quickly
    - Demonstrated interdependence of financial economies as effects were felt across the globe
  - ○ *Mutual interdependence* recognized
  - ○ 'Group of Seven'(US, Britain, France, Federal Republic of Germany, Italy, Canada, Japan) meet in annual economic summits since 1970
  - ○ Organization for Economic Cooperation and Development (OECD) brings leading industrialized nations together
  - ○ Developing nations still on economic periphery
- The Enlarged European Community: Problems and Opportunities
  - ○ European Community originally six
    - 1973: Britain, Denmark, Ireland added
    - 1981: Greece added
    - 1986: Spain and Portugal added
    - 1995: Austria, Finland, Sweden added
  - ○ *Growing pains* as diversity of the group made decisions difficult
    - Britain complained of paying a disproportionate share of the budget without commensurate benefits
    - Enthusiasm for close political integration dimmed

- ○ 1973: leaders meet on regular basis, presidency rotates between countries
- ○ 1979: election to European Parliament mainly symbolic
- <u>Toward a 'Single Europe' : The European Union</u>
- 'Third industrial revolution'
- Postindustrial age meant that sophisticated communication was the key to success
- 1977: first personal computer
- In terms of technology, Europeans were outdistanced for now by US and Japan because post-1974 recession made it difficult for Europeans to promote research/ development
- 1987: Single European Act: 12 member nations agree to establish common production standards, remove impediments to trade, common charter of labor rights
  - ○ Unified European currency projected for late 1990s
- Confirmed in Treaty of European Union signed at Maastricht in the Netherlands 1991
- European union becomes the largest trading block in the global economy
- Dangers of protectionism: industrial nations might divide into large regional trading blocs and new competitive barriers could interfere with free trade.
  - ○ Price and quality for consumer usually suffer under protectionism
- **THE COLD WAR REKINDLED**
- 1974 Nixon resigns due to Watergate scandal
- Ford succeeds him but ousted by Carter (Democrat) in 1977
- Carter administration concerned with human rights world-wide
- US will trade with USSR only if they permit freedom to dissenters, allow emigration for Soviet Jews and others, and end coercion of Poland
- Both countries continued strategic arms talks, sign SALT II treaty January 1979
- Soviet Union invades Afghanistan to support pro-Soviet regime
  - ○ Carter sees this as a huge threat to democracy and withdraws SALT II treaty before ratification
  - ○ Embargoes sales of grain and high technology to soviets, but European allies refused to support the embargo
  - ○ US will not send athletes to Olympics (to be held in USSR) in protest
  - ○ Afghanistan becomes a war of attrition for USSR like Vietnam (fought for a long time without tangible gains)
- In addition to economic problems, Carter was facing the problem of hostages in Iran
  - ○ Ayatollah Ruhollah Khomeini overthrows pro-western Shah in 1979
  - ○ Iranians take American embassy personnel hostage
  - ○ Failed rescue attempt by US, so Carter lost popularity

- <u>The Reagan Years: From Revived Cold War to New Détente</u>
- Reagan called the Soviet Union an 'evil empire', pledged to restore America's prestige
- Increased defense appropriations, military spending, *confrontational stand against communism*
  - Afghanistan: increased arms shipments to guerillas and Pakistan
  - Poland: economic sanctions when it imposed martial law in '81 (under Soviet pressure) to suppress Solidarity trade union movement
  - Soviets: reinforced embargo on sale of high technology
  - Accused Soviets of using Castro's regime in Cuba and Sandinista regime in Nicaragua to spread communism in Latin America
  - Supported authoritarian governments as long as they were anti-communist, believing they that these countries could later be democratized while communism was intractable
- Reagan's policy in Middle East
- Libya: bombed military installation in retaliation for Libyan supported terrorist activities
- Code-named Operation *El Dorado Canyon*; air-strikes against Libya on April 15, 1986. in response to a Berlin discotheque bombing which targeted American servicemen.
  - Gaddafi was firmly anti-Israel and had supported extremist groups in Palestine and Syria.
  - Libya was attempting to become a nuclear power and had occupied Chad
- 1982 Lebanon: Following the invasion of Lebanon by Israel, Reagan sent 800 Marines to join a multinational force to oversee the evacuation of Palestinian guerrillas from Beirut.
  - The force remained—in support of the fragile pro-western government—thereby identifying itself with one of the factions in the country's long and bloody civil war, which had begun in 1975.
  - On the morning of October 23, 1983, two suicide bomber/trucks drove into the Marine's and French compounds
    - Killed 299 American and French military
    - The blasts led to the withdrawal of the international peacekeeping force
    - The organization Islamic Jihad claimed responsibility for the bombing.
- In war between Iran and Iraq, US intent on asserting American leadership and keeping the Soviets out of the Middle East
- <u>Nuclear Arms Control</u>
- The ultimate threat of nuclear war hung over every crisis
- 1952: US developed hydrogen bomb

- 1960s: both developed long range missiles capable of accurately delivering nuclear warheads across the globe
- New age of military technology
- 1963: partial test-ban treaty (only underground testing was allowed, not in the atmosphere)
- 1968: Nonproliferation treaty endorsed by UN General Assembly and signed by 130+ states, but was ignored as more countries developed nuclear power
- Accidents: Three Mile Island and Chernobyl
- Mutually assured destruction (MAD), or "balance of terror"
  - Each side had enough weapons to destroy each other multiple times: overkill
  - Continued to modernize at exorbitant costs and kept developing new weapons
- End of 1980s: both sides had satellite reconnaissance systems and over 25,000 nuclear weapons
- Fear of attack due to miscommunication led to installation of a hot line between Kremlin and White House.
- Security debates went back and forth: some urged unilateral disarmament, but some said without high level of armaments a country could be nuclear blackmailed
- **CHINA AFTER MAO**
- Mao died in 1976 and a competition between radical and moderate communist factions ensued
- His widow, Jiang Qing sought leadership but failed and was imprisoned
- Deng Xiaoping, leader of moderates, emerged in '77
- He had fallen out of favor with Mao in '56, purged for taking the 'capitalist road'
- Deng's Reforms
- De-emphasized Marxist ideology
- Focused on economic growth and modernization
- Without abandoning socialism, sanctioned capitalist practices
  - New economic system a 'marriage' between both a planned and a market economy
  - Allowed cultivation of land by individual farmers
  - Small business in private hands
  - Opened the country to foreign investment
- Welcomes western science/technology/management techniques
- Gross domestic product grew by 9% annually
- Many new entrepreneurs became wealthy
- People's Liberation Army: reduced in size, modernized, more professional

- Individual human rights frequently violated but still more open and relaxed atmosphere prevailed
- Western culture more readily accepted
- Wished to have an orderly succession, dislodged veterans of old generation and allowed for younger leaders to emerge
- Economic difficulties emerged
- Rapid economic growth fueled inflation
- Rising levels of consumption strained resources
- Erratic price control encouraged black market
- Consumer society bred extravagance
- Corruption became widespread
- 1988: Deng calls for entrenchment and pause in reform
- Could have been more successful if not for the rejection of democracy
- Young people pressed for a loosening of the party's political controls, a freer press, and the right to criticize the government
- **The 'Democracy Movement'**
  - 1986: Hu Yaobang encouraged the belief that greater political freedom might be permitted
- Students took to the streets in support
- Hu was replaced, this set off demonstrations demanding democracy in Tiananmen Square
  - Students across the country joined the 'democracy movement'
  - Zhao Ziyang, Hu's replacement, pressed for conciliation but Deng wouldn't allow it
  - Government imposed martial law, and when students refused to leave the square, they opened fire killing hundreds
  - Deng's popularity plummeted, and a repressive atmosphere followed
  - Deng attributed the demonstrations to a 'western inspired conspiracy' saying the students wanted capitalism in China so it would be dependent on other countries
  - The democracy movement showed how powerful the pressures for political change were in China
  - Deng's successor Jiang Zemin relatively moderate
    - Pursued goals of modernization
    - Sought reconciliation with the west
    - Wanted economic ties with the west, but criticized by them due to China's poor record on human rights
  - Population Growth

157

- Pressure of expanding population on the economy remained serious
- Chinese government policy focused in coping with population growth
- One-child-per-family rule (Still difficult because rich families were willing to pay the fine for having more than one child and contraceptives were not very modern or effective)
- Massive education programs combined with social & government pressure (ostracized by neighbors, denial of government benefits)

- China had become a regional superpower and nuclear power. It remained under a tight authoritarian and Marxist regime, contrasting the rest of the world where Communist regimes of the Cold War era were disappearing

CHAPTER 15

COLLAPSE OF THE USSR & FACING THE 21st CENTURY

The Crisis in the Soviet Union

- Mikhail S. Gorbachev
    - ○ Studied agriculture in Stavropol (home town in southwest Russia)
    - ○ Became party secretariat in Moscow in 1978 (special responsibility for agriculture)
    - ○ 1980- member of Politburo
    - ○ By 1984 he was being trained for party leadership
    - ○ "...nice smile, but he's got iron teeth"- Gromyko
    - ○ Following the death of Chernenko in 1985, Gorbachev was appointed General Secretary of the party despite being the youngest member of the Politburo

- *Perestroika*
    - ○ Drastic modification of centrally planned economy inherited from Stalin, and passed down trough many Soviet Leaders
    - ○ Industry and agriculture needed freedom from restraints to release creative energies, provide incentives for productivity, raise quality levels, and satisfy consumer needs
    - ○ Proposed remedy of decentralization, self-management for industry and agriculture, end to bureaucracy, and incentives for productivity

- *Glasnost*
    - ○ "Openness" closely linked to economic reform
    - ○ Meant the right to voice the need for change, freedom to criticize existing system, and willingness to reexamine wrongdoings
    - ○ Led to unprecedented liberalization of Soviet society, free press, and an end to totalitarian control of everyday life
    - ○ Led to publishing of *Dr. Zhivago* (Pasternak) and *Gulag Archipelago* (Solzhenitsyn)

- o KGB came under scrutiny (although remained a powerful force to be reckoned with)
- 1987- Gorbachev denounced Stalin's crimes; monument to his victims is planned
- Constitutional reforms in 1988 created Congress of People's Deputies
- Individuals encouraged to form businesses and cooperatives
  - o Foreign capital and investment was now welcome
  - o However, many reforms were blocked by government bureaucrats as they only existed on paper
- Agriculture
  - o Gorbachev's reforms on agriculture fell short of what was needed
  - o Production did not rise
  - o State remained legal owner of land
  - o Little more that 1% of land shifted to private hands
- March 1989-multiparty candidate elections were held
- On 15 March 1990, Gorbachev was elected as the first executive President of the Soviet Union with broad executive powers
  - o The country remained divided between those who resisted changes, and a growing group of democratic reformers who wanted more for Gorbachev
  - o Azerbaijan and Armenia fought over a disputed enclave
  - o Violence in Georgia
  - o The 15 constituent Republics of Soviet Union demand independence
  - o Three Baltic states: Latvia, Lithuania, Estonia in turmoil, also wanted independence
    - ▪ The "Baltic Way: In the late 1980s a massive campaign of civil resistance against the Soviets: the Singing revolution.
    - ▪ A human chain of two million stretched for 600 km from Tallinn to Vilnius on August 23, 1989.
    - ▪ The secession of the Baltic republics from the USSR had become inevitable.
    - ▪ This process contributed to the dissolution of the Soviet Union and set a precedent for the other Soviet republics to secede
    - ▪ The Soviet Union recognized the independence of the three Baltic states on September 6, 1991
- Gorbachev believed the highest concern should be human rights
- Gorbachev changed the image of the Soviet Union as a military threat and promoter of world revolution; became more democratic and peaceful
- Détente and arms reduction were essential to relieve military burned on economy
- Gorbachev meets with Reagan in 1987, consent to remove the intermediate-range missiles each had installed in Europe, agree to reduce long-range missiles

- 1991-Gorbachev and Bush agree to scale down about a third of its arsenal of long-range nuclear missiles
- Gorbachev commits to withdrawal of Soviet troops from Afghanistan ("bleeding wound")
- The Collapse of Communism in Central and Eastern Europe
- Dissidents called for recognition of civil rights promised in Helsinki accords
- State-run monopolies went unchallenged
- Eastern European countries were heavily in debt (Poland owed about ½ of total amount)
- Poland
    - Gomulka disappointed reformers
    - Oust Gomulka in 1970 due to riots over food prices, in comes Edmund Gierek
    - 1980 rise in food prices led to strikes
    - Solidarity-independent trade union federation
        - National symbol of protest in Poland = Lech Walesa
        - Solidarity (a union not sanctioned by communist government) has 10 million members
            - Call for free elections and role of Solidarity in government
    - Government ousts Gierek and puts in Jaruzelski
        - 1981-imposes marital law, banned Solidarity
    - John Paul II- first Polish pope to head the Roman catholic church (1978), inspired demonstration during a visit to Poland
    - Lech Walesa wins Nobel Peace Prize in 1993
    - 1989- communist government permits parliamentary elections
        - New government moved towards free market economy
    - Lech Walesa elected president in 1990
- Hungary
    - 1988-oust hard-lined dictator Kadar
    - Dissolved Communist party
    - Reassert national independence, restored self-government and civic freedom, open way to market-oriented economy and pluralist democracy
    - September 1989-Hungary opened border with Austria and allowed Germans to exit
- German Democratic Republic: Revolution and Reunification
    - Erich Honecker, in power since 1961, held the line against reform
    - Berlin Wall-built in 1961

- o East Germans began to flee the German Democratic Republic for Federal Republic of Germany
- o Leipzig-over 100,000 demonstrators marched for an end to police state, forced Honecker to resign
- o November 9, 1989-Berlin wall falls
- o The entire party came crashing down, young reformers assumed control
- o Pressure for reunification built initiated by Christian Democratic chancellor Helmut Kohl
  - ▪ Allies feared a united Germany due to the past
  - ▪ Four powers decided to relinquish occupation rights and in 1990 the two states formally united to become an enlarged Federal Republic of Germany
  - ▪ Western Deutsche Mark became official currency
  - ▪ Capital re-established at Berlin (no longer Bonn)
  - ▪ The fusion of the two states made currency unstable, risked inflation stemming from the absorption of East Germany's decayed economy.
- Czechoslovakia
  - o Charter '77-organization of intellectuals formed after the Helsinki accords rallied against dictatorship
  - o Reformers came together, inspired by leadership of writer Vaclav Havel
  - o Demonstrators demanded an end to party-state dictatorship
  - o Havel became president
  - o The "velvet" revolution: nonviolent
  - o Czechoslovakia had strongest democratic sentiment
  - o Fell apart in 1993- Czech Republic and Slovakia
- Bulgaria
  - o Revolution was palace coup within the party
  - o Considered the most docile Soviet state
- Romania
  - o Nicolae Ceausescu controlled party and government
    - ▪ Stalin-like ambition
    - ▪ Dissent was controlled, built enormous palace
    - ▪ December 1989-protests in Timisoara, brutality against protestors sparked more anger
    - ▪ Ceausescu and wife were killed
    - ▪ National Salvation Front took over
  - o Was the most repressive dictatorship in Europe until 1989

- With the exception of Romania, all revolutions were peaceful!
- The Collapse of the Soviet Union
- 1990-production was in steep decline
- Gorbachev abandoned 500-Day economic plan that would have freed prices and moved more swiftly to a market economy
- Shevardnadze resigned
- January 1991 Soviet troops used military force against demonstrators in Lithuania
- Boris N. Yeltsin emerged
    - Had been party boss in Moscow
    - Member of Politburo
    - 1987-openly attacked party officials, was dismissed from his posts
    - Found allies among democratic reformers
    - Elected to Soviet legislature in 1989
    - 1990 became chairman of Russian Supreme Soviet
    - Became president in 1991 by popular vote to the newly created post of President of the Russian Soviet Federative Socialist Republic (SFSR)
        - At that time one of the 15 constituent republics of the Soviet Union
    - Demanded immediate independence for the Baltic states and self-government for Russia and of the Soviet constituent republics
- A small coterie of hard liners acted to seize power
    - Expected to be a small operation, but it failed
- Yeltsin denounced communist party
- Ukraine declared itself independent after the coup
- By 1922, the Soviet Union was dissolved
- Gorbachev resigned
- Commonwealth of Independent States
    - 1991
    - Made up of countries which were former Soviet Republics, formed during the breakup of the Soviet Union
- Russia took seat of Soviet Union in the UN
- Gorbachev failed in that he did not build a new system to replace the communism he undermined
- Russia, like other former Soviet republics, entered a period of difficult transition following the dissolution of the USSR.
    - The Russian Federation that emerged consisted of 21 "federated republics."
    - The most pressing challenge facing Yeltsin internationally was the issue of nuclear weaponry.

- He eventually worked out an agreement to retain nuclear weapons in Russia, though under mediation with the US, Russia began to dismantle its nuclear weapons under an arms reduction treaty.
  - Yeltsin also faced separatist threats, mainly in the threat of flaring violence and civil war.
  - Domestically, Yeltsin had to deal with economic issues.
    - The transition into a market economy was harsh and rocky—production declined and living standards sunk.
    - Corruption increased throughout the country.
  - A new Duma was created under Yeltsin and his new constitution, which gave extended powers to Yeltsin.
  - There was also threat of attack from Chechnya, which, taking advantage of the prior Soviet Union's weakness, demanded independence or equal partnership with Russia.
    - Guerrilla warfare broke out and the Russian resorted to air bombings of Chechnya.
- The Balkans
- The roots of ethnic and religious conflict in the Balkans stemmed from historical animosities
  - The nationalist sentiments of minorities were exploited by political leaders in the wake of communism's collapse.
  - Historically, the Balkans had been dominated by empires like Austria and the Ottoman Empire, or the Nazis during World War II.
    - Serbia, for example, had been conquered by the Ottoman Turks and later remained under Turkish rule until it gained independence.
    - Croatia and Slovenia had been ruled by the Ottomans, but later rejoined the Austrian Empire. During World War II, the Nazis invaded Yugoslavia and established Croatia as a puppet Nazi state.
  - After the collapse of communism, former Communist leaders in Serbia and Croatia put themselves at the head of nationalist crusades.
  - Open warfare eventually broke out in mid-1991. Serbs and Croats competed amongst themselves for territory, like in Bosnia.
  - The leader of the Serbian-Montenegrin crusade against Bosnia was Slobodan Milosevic.
- Although the international community limited in scope its intervention in the Balkans, it did contribute largely to the resolution of conflict.
  - One limitation was that the international community was unable even to deliver food and medical supplies to countries in need.
  - The UN and NATO, however, were able to mediate for the Balkans, leading to a cease-fire and diplomatic settlements for Bosnia.

- o Croats and Muslims also agreed to form a Croat-Muslim federation in the remains of Bosnian territory after Serb conquests.
- o New troubles arose, though, as Serbia was threatened by a separatist movement and Milosevic launched an offensive to wipe out the Kosovars, which the UN and NATO denounced.
- o In response to the continued offense, NATO launched an air bombing against Serbia until Milosevic yielded.
  - That summer, Kosovars returned under international protection.
- o Aside from Germany, many West Europeans remained unemployed.
  - Dissatisfaction with the political systems became widespread.
  - New parties emerged in Italy, like the Center-Right coalition and the Popular Party (formerly the Christian Democratic Party).
  - When Communist barriers collapsed, refugees from Eastern Europe and Yugoslavia flooded into Western Europe, taking "inferior" jobs that many Europeans did not want.
  - There was a general gloom and pessimism that enveloped West Europe after the Cold War ended, as economic instability reigned.
- Clinton took a new path in politics.
  - o He pursued a mixture of Democratic and Republican pro-business politics.
  - o He combined that pro-business tact with healthcare and welfare reforms for the poor and minorities.
  - o He was matched across the pond by the policies of Tony Blair who had similar pro business policies and total overhaul of welfare programs.
  - o Clinton's "third way" encouraged economic growth and the decline of the welfare state without pushing "pure selfish individualism" which was strongly criticized.
    - Market economy and private enterprise were encouraged greatly and were considered to be the productive forces that would ultimately benefit everyone by boosting the economy.
    - In England it became accepted that stability was not necessarily resisting change, as had been learned by resistance to Ireland's home rule.
- Religion in the Modern World
- 1978: John Paul II became 1st Polish Pope ever elected
  - o Encouraged Christian ecumenical movement
  - o Reached out to non-Christians as well (in Asia, Africa, Latin America)
  - o Diplomatic relations with USSR to improve status of the church
  - o Apologized for the abuses of the Crusades, Inquisition, ambivalence during the Holocaust
  - o When it came to the church, he favored orthodoxy and papal supremacy
    - Curbed assertiveness of national churches

- No marriage for clergy, no women as priests, no rights for divorce, homosexuality a sin
- This caused protest against "new Roman centralism" – church would not change central precepts, and wouldn't share authority

- Judaism still haunted by Holocaust
    - Jews everywhere (especially in US) lent support to state of Israel
    - Anti-Zionism was equated with anti-Semitism
    - The collapse of communism renewed anti-Semitism in Eastern Europe
- In some non-Western religions (Islam, Hinduism, Buddhism), modernization was rejected
- Many immigrants to W brought their faith with them!
- Rise of fundamentalism: militant religious reform movements
    - Rejected secularism, turned to literal translations of texts
    - Many militant regimes (ex: Sudan, Afghanistan)
    - Demanded unswerving adherence to sacred texts regardless of societal changes
    - Islam: The 1979 Islamic Revolution in Iran is seen by Western scholars the start of modern Islamic fundamentalism.
        - Post-1920s movements starting with the Muslim Brotherhood, are seen to practice "extremism"
    - Hindu extremism in India (violence against Indian Muslims, threatened by secular state)
    - also found in Christian and Jewish sects – counteracted blending of cultures (bred intolerance and separatism)
- Activism: The Youth Rebellion of the 1960s
    - For the first time, there was a true "youth culture"
        - Partly because of the 'baby boom', youngsters grew up with a new generational identity, both created by and a reflection of popular culture
        - 1960s: youth activism – worldwide student rebellion
            - Took for granted all the new science, technology, etc., and aware of the world's flaws
                - Partly inspired by cultural revolution in China
                - At the center was the United States and France
                - US: Hippie and antiwar
                - Both: near revolutionary in 1968
                - France: threatened to overthrow regime when 10 million workers went on strike
    - Militancy of students alienated many, and government restored order

- Some of earliest and largest demonstrations were in US because civil rights movements and anti-Vietnam war sentiment (assassinations of Martin Luther King, Jr., and Robert Kennedy also fueled anger)
- Students made heroes out of foes of established order: Castro, Ho Chi Minh, Mao Zedong, Malcolm X. Played into hands of Soviet bloc propaganda.
- Neo-Marxist philosopher: Herbert Marcuse believed that tolerance of bourgeois was a trap to prevent protest against society
- "New Left" believed revolutionary leadership would come from Maoist China and 3rd world (not USSR)
- "Destroy in order to purify"
- Rebellion faded by early 1970s
- In the US, helped to bring the Vietnam War to an end.

- The Women's Liberation Movement
- Militant phase began in US in mid 1960s (partly parallel to civil rights movement)
  - Inspired by books such as de Beauvoir's *The Second Sex* (France, 1949) and Friedan's *The Feminine Mystique* (US, 1963)
  - Legal discrimination was diminishing, but women still called for end to all economic and societal barriers
  - Many more women entered work force in 1970s
    - Women still denied many rights in many poorer countries, where opportunities for women (especially education) could accelerate social advances – UN tries to help
- UN affirms "universal rights of women" – discrimination occurred in both capitalist and socialist societies
  - More women had high political positions (example: Indira Ghandi, Margaret Thatcher)
- More sexual freedom – legalized abortion, birth control pill, etc.
- College attendance for women increasing
- Demands for equal compensation for work
- **FACING THE 21st CENTURY**
- New Configuration of World Affairs
- Peace and security are still most pressing problems (more conflicts within countries than between them)
- Rivalries between religion-based societies (not nation-states) are most important. Examples are Serbs vs. Croatians, and Israel vs. Arab world
- Religions divisive, and were still affected by secularism and globalization
- More people recognize global diversity
- UN represents an "international community", and membership continues expanding

- o New states demanded more authority in the General Assembly, which was often a forum for grievances of developing nations against wealthy industrial world
- Universal Declaration of Human Rights (adopted by UN in 1948) focused only on political and civil rights
  - o Some developing nations said these "rights" were actually Western ideas
    - An excuse for the excesses of authoritarian regimes
  - o Little desire to intervene in internal affairs of other people, but difficult to ignore violations of human rights
    - Increased ethnic and religious-based nationalism led to issues of humanitarian assistance and intervention (peacemaking vs. peacekeeping)
- US refused to place its own troops in UN peacekeeping forces; criticized UN's large bureaucracy
  - o UN often seen as powerless in large conflicts
  - o US was now the only superpower, and was called to exercise leading role in international affairs
    - Sometimes hard to distinguish US unilateralism from international action
    - 1992: first time US troops reinforce UN peacekeeping forces in Somalia (called by Clinton "assertive multilateralism"
    - In Oct. 1993, US troops were attacked by paramilitary Somali groups, and Congress now restricted these interventions
      - UN peacekeeping role was threatened (failure to help in Bosnia or Rwanda)
      - 1999: American air-led offensive by NATO in Yugoslavia set precedent for multinational humanitarian intervention
      - Definition of national interests remained unresolved (example: US and the Middle East)
      - increased military and defense role for EU, which should, according to French, be an equal partner and counterbalance to the hegemony of the US
      - Russia's new role was undefined: was still a power, but could not be involved in international affairs. Also the issue with Russia having large numbers of nuclear weapons
  - o NATO admitted Hungary, Poland, and Czech Republic in 1999, and planned to admit more formerly Soviet-controlled countries in central and east Europe
    - Distrust of Russian intentions by Eastern Europeans
    - Russia saw this as a provocation
      - US and Russia confirmed their commitment to the mutual reduction of long-range missiles

- May 2000, the five nuclear powers (US, Russia, Britain, France, China) pledged themselves to eventual elimination of all nuclear weapons
- Concerns because more nations were developing nuclear arms (India, Pakistan)
- US refuses to ratify Comprehensive Nuclear Test Ban Treaty in 1999. Believes that periodic testing of arsenals is in its national security.
- President George W. Bush's proposal to build missile defense shield against nuclear attack. Seen as setback by nuclear arms control advocates (because they were supposed to be reducing offensive weapons and banning building of defensive ones).
    - Relationship with People's Republic of China also very important: US still recognizes PRC but opposes forcible annexation of non-communist Taiwan.
- The Population Explosion
- Resulted from:
    - Medical discoveries, especially penicillin and "wonder drugs"
    - Improved health and sanitation measures,
    - Declining infant mortality,
    - More efficient food production (hybrids that yield more harvests than before) and distribution
- Contemporary "population explosion" began in 1950 with "baby boom"
- Growing exponentially, with a 2% annual growth rate
- Continuous debate exists over the earth's "carrying capacity"
- Growth rate showed signs of decline after 1965 due to a decrease in birth rate
    - Compared to developing nations, Europe and North America were experiencing a shrinking share of the world's population
    - Nonetheless, population growth still threatened to cancel economic advances of developing nations
- Some religions ban use of contraceptives, or restrict education and job opportunities for women
- The Environment
- From 1950 to 2000, the world industrial production grew fivefold
- Scientists believe emissions are harming ozone layer
- High levels of industrial pollution worldwide (severe environmental damage in former USSR)
- Plant and animal species were endangered, especially in Latin American and Africa
- 1970s: began talk of sustainable economic growth rates: growth could be maintained without destruction of humanity's natural habitat
- Alternative forms of energy: sun, wind, nuclear
- US Environmental Protection Agency established in 1970

- 1992: first "Earth Summit" meeting in Rio de Janeiro; 178 nations pledge to protect plant and animal life, and halt global warming
- "Green" political parties emerged

ABOUT THE AUTHOR

Dr. Juan R. Céspedes is a veteran educator, lecturer, and author. Born in Havana, Cuba, he fled with his family from the Castro-communist dictatorship to the United States. For nearly three decades Dr. Céspedes has shared his thoughts and research about history, politics, economics, and international relations with a wide audience. He is the author of *Collapse of the Soviet Empire*, and *War Interminable: The Origins, Causes, Practices and Effects of International Conflict*. An advocate of individual freedom, human dignity and democratic government, he has traveled widely, studied, and reported extensively on major topics such as the nature of totalitarian regimes, the Cold War, the causes of wars, and the history of terrorism. Dr. Céspedes began his career studying economics and labor relations at Florida International University, where he obtained a Bachelor of Science Degree in Industrial Technology. Subsequently, he obtained a Master of Science Degree in Gifted Education from Nova Southeastern University, and a Ph.D. in Education and Leadership from Barry University. He is currently a History Instructor for the International Baccalaureate program at Miami-Dade County Public Schools, an Examiner for the International Baccalaureate Organization, and Adjunct Professor at Barry University. He believes that a 21st century history education needs a comprehensive view where the learner becomes an analyst conscientious of social, economic, cultural, political and other human conditions. For Dr. Céspedes, historical analysis does not imply revisionism with preconceived ideas of what "should have been," nor assumptions made from a modern-day perspective. His extensive and detailed work not only endows us with a historical documentation of human triumph and accomplishment, but also makes us aware of our failures, cruelty, and sometimes our inhumanity toward each other. Dr. Céspedes believes that "A true understanding of history is the basis for appreciating the human condition and grappling with the moral issues facing a democratic society today."

Made in the USA
Charleston, SC
21 April 2012